Angling Entomology

BASICS
for Fly Fishermen

6-14-89

RON MOSER

Angling Entomology

BASICS
for Fly Fishermen

Ron Moser

Photographs by the author
Illustrated by R. Mark Heath

Nick Lyons Books

Copyright © 1987 by Ron Moser

ALL RIGHTS RESERVED. No part of this book may be reproduced in any manner without the express written consent of the publisher, except in the case of brief excerpts in critical reviews and articles. All inquiries should be addressed to: Nick Lyons Books, 31 West 21 Street, New York, NY 10010.

PRINTED IN THE UNITED STATES OF AMERICA

10 9 8 7 6 5 4 3 2 1

Library of Congress Cataloging-in-Publication Data

Moser, Ron.
  Angling entomology.

  Bibliography: p.
  Includes index.
  1. Insects, Aquatic. 2. Fly fishing. I. Title.
SH456.M67   1987   799.1'2   87-3220
ISBN 0-941130-34-7

Contents

Fisherman's Foreword	vi
Entomologist's Foreword	vii
1 Getting Started	11
2 Insects	14
3 Collecting, Rearing, and Preserving Insects	54
4 Data Collecting and Recording	75
Glossary	84
Bibliography	90
Biological Supply Houses	93
Index	94

Acknowledgments

So many people have contributed to the production of this book that attempting to credit each person individually would be impossible. The contributions of two people, however, demand specific recognition. So, to all the fly fishermen, angling authors, and others whose work is reflected in this book, and in particular to Robert L. Brown for his many hours of invaluable assistance in the field, and to R. Mark Heath for his very imaginative and original artwork, my deepest appreciation.

*To my wife, JANET LEE,
with all my love and respect
for her patience, understanding, and encouragement*

Fisherman's Foreword

I think that secretly every fly fisherman who fishes for trout would like to know a little more about what trout eat: the insects, where they live, how they develop and behave, and a dozen other facts that would help them catch more fish. Applying even the most basic understanding of insect forms and behavior to pattern selection and presentation will make *any* fly fisherman a more successful angler. The problem is that most books, to the novice, seem highly technical, are often dull, and frequently go far beyond the angler's true needs.

Ron Moser's *Angling Entomology: Basics for Fly Fishermen* is a small book with a huge amount of information that is practical and easily absorbed. Ron takes you by the hand, and if you've never looked under a rock in the stream, he'll show you how you can easily sort out, recognize, and study the insect species that you'll need to know to catch more trout on the waters you fish.

This is by far the best book I've read if you want to get to know the various insects of fly-fishing importance. The writing style and illustrations in this book are so easy to understand that I'm convinced any trout fisherman can, in a short time, vastly increase his knowledge of angling entomology—a subject that is sure to help him catch more fish.

—Lefty Kreh

Entomologist's Foreword

Ron Moser is an interesting character.

A few years ago he walked into my office looking for some vials to put "some aquatics I caught in alcohol." His technical knowledge of insects was limited to some observations he made while fishing. I am, unfortunately, not a fisherman, but an entomologist, but I was greatly impressed by the enthusiasm and desire for knowledge shown by Ron.

We discussed aquatic insects and I figured that would be the end of it. To my surprise, Ron was back next week, with his new "catch," plus loads of questions. Overnight he had become fascinated with the study of insects and, in the typical Ron Moser fashion, had delved deeply and thoroughly into the subject. As Ron studied, read, and observed, he realized how much was being missed by people engaging in his favorite sport.

This book is the result of his efforts to help his fellow fishermen. The book is technically correct, extremely well written, and a pleasure to read. Ron has managed to bridge the gap between the entomological scientist and the pragmatic fisherman. He has clearly shown the way to improve fishing techniques by explaining in a clear and lucid manner the "how, what, where, and why" of insects in relation to fish behavior.

It gives me great satisfaction and pleasure to have been asked to write this foreword. I am sure the reader will find the book both entertaining and educational. It may cause you to pick up an insect net—as it has made me want to pick up a fly rod.

—Eugene J. Gerberg
Ph.D., R.P.E.

1

Getting Started

If you're like many anglers who have decided to learn something about insects of fly-fishing importance, you're probably not quite sure what that will involve, or how difficult it may be. There's no reason to be concerned. For those interested only in fundamentals, studying angling entomology simply involves collecting some information about certain insects and the environments they inhabit that can later be applied when fishing. And no one will have any problem understanding or applying the concepts and procedures described in this book.

One of the objectives I set for myself when I began writing this little book was to make its use as easy and enjoyable as possible. Toward that end, the text has been organized into building blocks; the information in one block serves as a foundation for understanding that contained in succeeding blocks. Beyond that, and the fact that it's written in conversational English, the material in this book has been very narrowly focused. Instead of attempting to discuss everything that's known about angling entomology, this book addresses only three basic, but very important, questions. They are

• Regardless of geographic location, time of year, type of water fished, or angling abilities, what must a fly fisherman have learned about the basics of angling entomology *before going into the field?*
• What must a fly fisherman *take into the field* in order to collect needed reference materials and record essential data?
• What kinds of equipment and supplies should a fly fisherman *have at home* in order to pursue the study of angling entomology?

Before we begin addressing these questions, however, there are a few other points I want to mention.

First, the end product of having studied angling entomology is knowledge or data. Unfortunately, because of the wealth of insect data available, one of the first problems confronting fly fishermen new to angling entomology is trying to decide what's really *important?* In this regard, and because this book deals only with basics, "important" will mean insect and related information that's of *immediate and practical angling value.*

Second, while this may be your first reference dealing with angling entomology, it's not apt to be your last. Consequently, and to help you get started in your search for more advanced references, I've provided a short list of some specific works in the Bibliography that you may wish to examine.

Third, although this is a nontechnical reference, I nonetheless want to provide you with an opportunity to begin familiarizing yourself with a few basic technical terms in a way that shouldn't disturb your study of fundamentals. To accomplish this, from here on you'll periodically find numbered symbols like [§1], [§2] at the end of some sentences. They'll indicate you've just read a word, phrase, or whole paragraph which, in more advanced references, would have involved using technical terms. By matching the symbols in the text with their twins in the Glossary, you'll find some of that terminology. *Let me emphasize, however, that using this matching system is strictly optional!* If you want to ignore the symbols entirely, fine. But studying angling entomology is like eating salted peanuts. Once you've begun, it's almost impossible to quit! As a consequence, the sooner you begin acquainting yourself with some basic technical terms, the better. If you do decide to use the matching system, *don't* try matching any terms found in subsequent chapters with their counterparts in the Glossary until you've completed studying the entire chapter in which a symbol appears. Delaying matching will minimize any confusion you might otherwise encounter.

Finally, and most important, keep in mind that the practical value of your having studied angling entomology doesn't depend on how much information you gather about insects. Instead, it depends on your ability to draw conclusions of angling significance from your data, and to apply those conclusions when fly fishing. Given this, as you study the material that follows, try to resist the tendency simply to collect facts. Instead, as you review the concepts and procedures, ask yourself:

- "How can I use this information?"
- "Is this information I can use in connection with other data I've collected?"
- "Do I need to be on the lookout for more data in order to use this information?"

Said differently, if you really want to benefit from studying angling entomology, *think application!*

All right, with those brief introductory comments out of the way, let's talk about insects of fly-fishing importance!

2

Insects

I'm not sure whether the saying "10 percent of the anglers catch 90 percent of the fish" is true or not. I'm certain, however, that freshwater fly fishermen who have learned to apply a basic understanding of insect forms and behavior to pattern selections and presentations are far more successful anglers than those who haven't. To help you develop and apply that kind of understanding, let's consider insects of fly-fishing importance from several perspectives. Specifically, we'll discuss:

• Some of the physical and behavioral characteristics of insects in four different groups or *orders* of special interest to anglers;
• How to select insects for study that will complement your current and future fly-fishing skills and interests;
• Several different insect forms;
• Some of the habitats in which insects of fly-fishing importance are found and develop;
• Two methods of insect identification.

Insects

PERSONALIZING YOUR STUDY

Fly fishermen are usually anxious to try almost anything that might make them more successful anglers. But studying thousands of insects isn't one of those things. Anglers need only know certain things about certain insects. But because the insect interests of anglers differ, one of the first things you must learn is how to select insects for study that might be of fly-fishing importance to *you*. This isn't difficult. It involves "personalizing" your selection. And this can be accomplished by applying common sense and an understanding of your own fly-fishing skills and interests to answer six questions.

Is this insect commonly found in areas where the water I fish is located? To interest fish inhabiting the water you "work," an insect must obviously be available.

Is this insect going to be available when I plan to fish? Some insects are only available for a few days or weeks during the year, and then, sometimes, for only a few hours each day.

Is this an insect that develops in water? Is it often found in or on the water, or does it come close enough to the water to be captured by fish? Many insects, while available, aren't accessible to fish.

Will the fish I'm after recognize this insect as an important food source? Some insects that are both available and accessible to fish aren't considered "food." Of those that are, many aren't found in sufficient numbers to be considered important either by fish or fly fishermen.

Will I feel comfortable fishing a pattern matching the size of this insect? Many insects that are important food sources for fish are best imitated using patterns ranging from #16 to #28. Insects of this size won't be of immediate interest to those fly fishermen who will only fish patterns #14 or larger.

Can I use the fishing methods needed to present

effectively the patterns designed to imitate this insect? Insect forms dictating the use of weighted patterns or sinking lines won't be of immediate concern to anglers equipped only to fish floating patterns—or who, by preference, only fish dry flies.

You won't be able to answer all these questions right now. But by the time you've finished this book, done some insect collecting, and perhaps talked to other fly fishermen experienced in applying the basics of angling entomology on the water *you* fish, you'll have the information needed, or know where and how to find it.

But even without answers, some important concepts can be highlighted using these questions. For example, to be of truly practical value, the answers to the questions dealing with insect population characteristics—their size, makeup, and locations—should be "water specific" and reflect data collected on a particular piece of water at some particular site and time. The answers to questions dealing with insect and pattern forms and sizes, or the selection of fishing methods should reflect your current fly-fishing skills and interests in order to define certain criteria you'll need in connection with your study efforts. The answers to some questions may change over time. For example, a "no" today to questions related to insect or pattern forms and sizes may become a "yes" tomorrow if you learn new fishing methods or become more adept at employing those with which you're already familiar. "Personalizing" their selection will significantly reduce the number of insects you'll initially need or want to study. Indeed, instead of having to consider thousands of insects, many fly fishermen beginning the study of angling entomology and concerned only with basics often focus their attention on fewer than a dozen. Finally, the practical value of studying angling entomology depends largely on developing a working knowledge of the insect populations inhabiting the water *you* fish, when *you* plan to fish it.

INSECTS IN GENERAL

Insects are animals. They are found in many places, they vary in shape, size, and color, and they exhibit a wide variety of behaviors. Notwithstanding these differences, however, *all* insects of concern to fly fishermen:

- Complete their immature development either on land or in water, even though at different stages in their lives or under different circumstances they may be found in both environments;
- Have *life cycles* containing several developmental stages;
- Have bodies divided into three distinct regions—a head, thorax, and abdomen. (Depending on an individual insect's type or *species* and its stage of development, various structural features may be associated with each of these regions; [§1 through §5]
- Have skeletons on the *outside* of their bodies, which serve as a kind of "skin"; [§6]
- Exhibit radical changes in appearance and behavior as they develop.

Additionally, they may:

- Vary in length from a fraction of an inch to several inches;
- Have subdued or brilliant colors;
- Transport themselves by creeping, crawling, jumping, swimming, flying, or some combination of these methods.

These generalizations raise a point that can't be overemphasized. If there's one word that characterizes insects of fly-fishing interest, it's *variability*. In this regard, terms like "generally," "usually," and "may" are often used in

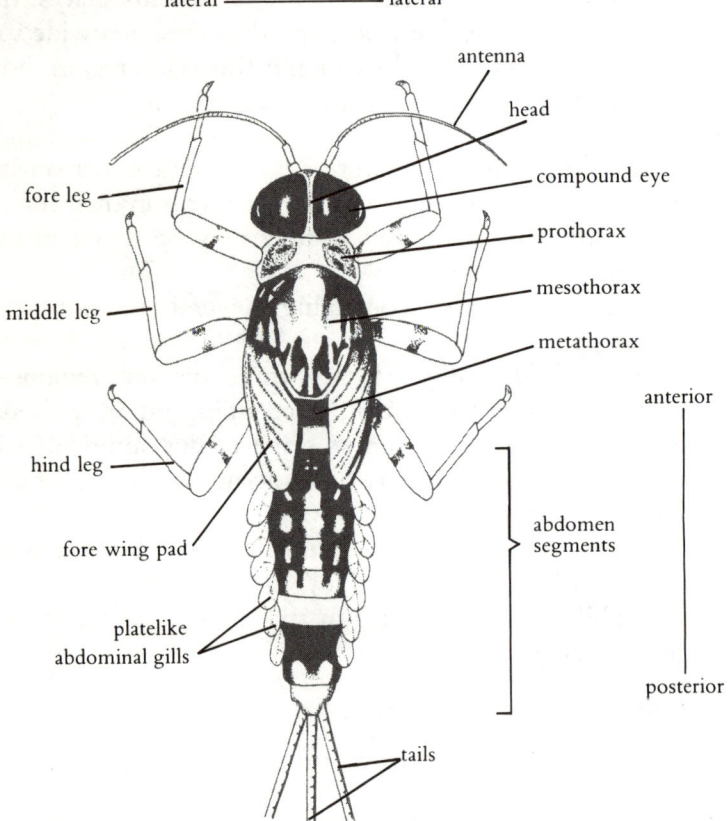

The Basic Structure of Insects

this book to indicate that there are exceptions to the point being discussed that would be examined in more detail in advanced works.

HABITATS

Given they've been learning to adapt for millions of years, it's hardly surprising that insects can be seen almost anywhere. But fly fishermen studying angling entomology must know more than just where insects can be found; they must also learn something about where insects develop.

Insects whose entire immature development occurs on land are called *terrestrial* insects. Some common *terrestrials* are ants, grasshoppers, and beetles. Some typical terrestrial habitats include:

- Patches of grass or weedy areas;
- Trees and shrubbery;
- Mounds of leaf mold or other decaying vegetation;
- Ant hills, bee hives, or other nests from which insects emerge.

While terrestrial habitats undoubtedly abound in areas surrounding the water you fish, to be of angling interest they must be located close enough to the water so that their occupants can transport themselves or be transported to it. In this regard, it's been the uncertainty about their accessibility, more than any question of their availability, that has tended to downgrade the importance of terrestrials in the minds of many fly fishermen. It's unfortunate this has happened, because at various times—especially during the summer—the availability and accessibility of terrestrial insects may produce some of the most exciting fly fishing you can encounter.

Insects whose entire immature development occurs in water are called *aquatic* insects. Some aquatic insects of particular fly-fishing significance include *stoneflies, mayflies, caddisflies,* and a small two-winged fly called a *midge.* Some common aquatic habitats include:

- Areas containing aquatic vegetation;
- Deposits of damp or water-covered sand, fine gravel, or silt;
- Collections of rocks at the heads, tails, or along the edges of lakes, pools, and runs;
- Stony riffles;
- Submerged debris, including broken tree limbs and collections of sticks or dead leaves;
- Spring and seepage pools.

Aquatic habitats should be of particular interest to you because in such habitats the insects that are most easily accessible to fish are found and develop.

A transitional zone in which land and water meet or overlap separates the areas generally inhabited by terrestrial or aquatic insects. It's a zone in which the terrestrials that interest fly fishermen are most often found. It's a zone toward which some immature aquatic insects migrate in preparation for taking flight. It's also a zone that will warrant special attention when you begin collecting insects. Some insect habitats typically found in a transitional zone include:

- Collections of rocks at or just above a waterline;
- Tree branches, shrubs, or other objects extending outward from the shoreline and over the water;
- Undercut stream, river, or lakeshore banks;
- Structures in or near the water;
- Vegetation extending above a waterline.

Before moving on, there are two more points about insect habitats worth mention. First, aquatic insects of a particular order or species are often attracted to habitats having certain physical characteristics. For example, large stoneflies prefer habitats that are constantly "flushed" with highly oxygenated water. Given that habitat preferences exist, and that the appearance and behavior of insects can vary, that the nature and extent of these variations can be extreme, and that these variations must be considered whenever making pattern selection and presentation decisions, it's critical that, as you fish, you look for changes in the habitat-types over which you're working that may signal the need to employ different pattern forms or fishing methods. Second, and equally important, it's essential that you remember that while immature and adult aquatic insects frequently go "ashore" by intent and are often collected there, any terrestrials found in the water probably got there by accident. We'll discuss the fly-fishing implications of this point in more detail when we address pattern presentations.

AQUATIC INSECTS

Fly fishermen have studied insects that develop in water for centuries. These efforts have produced mounds of information regarding their forms and behavior. Our discussion of aquatic insects, however, will be limited to a brief review of certain aspects of their life cycles and some of their more important physical and behavioral characteristics.

LIFE CYCLES

Like many other animals, aquatic insects hatch from

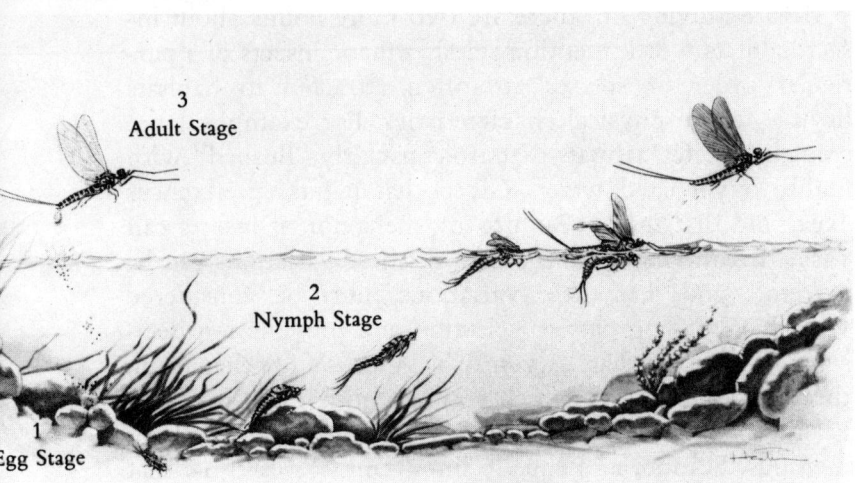

Aquatic Insect Life Cycle "A"

eggs, mature, reproduce, age, and die. That these major life-cycle events are repeated *in the same order at relatively fixed time intervals* is especially significant. It means that barring some radical man-made or natural change in the environment, once an aquatic insect population has been located and the shapes, sizes, colors, and behavior of its occupants noted, you can reasonably *predict* that insects having the *same* physical and behavioral characteristics will be found in approximately the *same* place at the *same* time next year and in subsequent years. More important from an angling perspective, once the patterns and presentations necessary to imitate effectively the forms and behavior of those insects have been identified, those same patterns and fishing methods should also generate strikes at approximately the *same* place and *same* time next year, and thereafter.

The accompanying figures depict two different aquatic insect life cycles. One or the other of these cycles applies to each aquatic insect order. Note that:

Insects

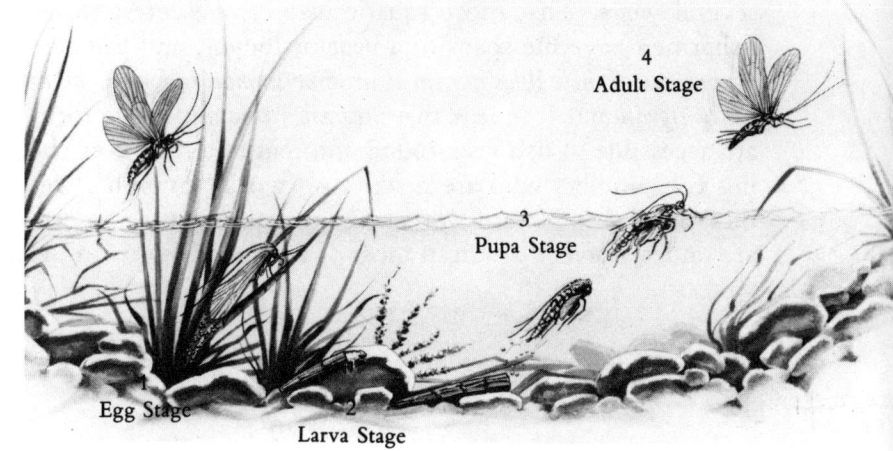

Aquatic Insect Life Cycle "B"

• Both cycles "A" and "B" contain *egg, nymphal or larval,* and *adult* stages. (The term *nymph* will be used in this book when referring to the *second* stage of development for insects having *three* stages in their life cycles—stoneflies and mayflies. The term *larva* (the plural form of this term is *larvae)* will apply to the *second* developmental stage of insects having *four* stages in their life cycles—caddisflies and midges [§7 and §8];

• An additional developmental stage, a *pupal* stage, is found only in cycle "B" [§9];

• Egg, nymphal, larval, and pupal stages relate to immature insect development that usually occurs under water;

• Except for mayflies in their semi-adult form, only aquatic insects in their adult stages are capable of flight;

• Only adult aquatic insects can reproduce.

Time must be considered in any discussion of life cycles. And depending on order, species, and other factors, the life spans of aquatic insects may range from a few days to several years. That most aquatic insects of interest to fly fishermen have life spans of a year or longer, and *that over 90 percent of their lives are spent in some immature form is especially significant.* It means that aquatic insects in some form are accessible to fish year-round and that in terms of catching fish, anglers who are unable to "work" nymphs, wet flies, and other patterns imitating immature aquatic insects are under a severe handicap most of the time they're on the water.

DEVELOPMENTAL STAGES

Aquatic insect life cycles "A" and "B" each contain several developmental stages. And when you begin applying your knowledge of angling entomology, the changes in insect forms and behaviors associated with these stages will be one of the most important factors you must consider whenever making pattern selection and presentation decisions.

The Egg Stage

Aquatic insects hatch from eggs laid by adult females of a previous generation [§10]. Eggs may be layed on, in, or under the water, or on vegetation, soil, or structures located near the water. The eggs themselves may be deposited singly, in clusters or "sacks," or in strings. While a microscopic examination of eggs laid by aquatic insects of different orders would reveal structural differences, these variations are of no importance for anglers studying the basics of angling entomology.

The Nymphal or Larval Stage

In the second stage of their development—the nymphal or larval stage—the differences in the physical and behavioral characteristics of aquatic insects that interest fly fishermen begin to appear.

The shapes, sizes, and colors of the nymphs or larvae in any single aquatic insect order can vary. Because these variations can be extreme, the pattern selection implications of each must be examined very carefully. But before doing so, the different ways in which immature aquatic insects accommodate growth during their development must be considered because size, shape, and color are affected by growth.

Look at these photographs carefully. They depict specimens of a single stonefly species at three successive points of nymphal development. Note that while the overall appearance of these insects has remained essentially unchanged, they obviously differ in size. While this might seem odd given that the skeletons of insects are on the outside of their bodies and, though flexible, don't stretch in the sense that rubber does, there's nothing mysterious about it. Like snakes, immature stoneflies, mayflies, cad-

A Caddisfly

disflies, and midges molt or cast their skin as they grow [§11 and §12]. Because the discarded skins that are evidence of their final molt can often be found attached to rocks and trees located near water, and because finding such evidence signals their probable accessibility, let's consider the case of molting stoneflies in more detail.

As the nymphs of stoneflies grow, a point is reached where internal forces cause the skin above the head and thorax to split, allowing the still-maturing insect to escape.

A Stonefly

Once free of its old skin, a stonefly's new, soft, and colorless skin will stretch, allowing for growth. Within minutes, however, the new skin will begin to "color up" and toughen to form a new skeleton. This molting process will be repeated many times during a stonefly's underwater development, with a final nymph-to-adult molt occurring after a stonefly leaves the water.

The molting process for mayfly nymphs is essentially the same as that for stoneflies except that some mayfly species complete their nymph-to-flying-insect molt while still in the water, and that the final molt of any mayfly is always from a nymph-to-semi-adult-insect form.

While midge and caddisfly larvae also cast their skins to accommodate growth, another factor must be considered before their transformation into flying insects can be discussed.

During their second stage of development, caddisfly larvae occupy or construct habitats having some very unusual features. Some habitats, like the crevasses between small rocks, are "fixed" in place but are modified to meet a particular insect's need. For example, the caddisfly larvae of one species construct nets across the upstream openings of such crevasses to capture food. Other caddisfly habitats are "portable" and are built by larvae that anglers often refer to as "case-makers." When a case-maker is undisturbed, it projects its head and thorax from its case and, using its legs, carries the case about as it forages for food. When disturbed, it withdraws its body into its case for protection. Depending on species, the extent of larval development, and habitat features, the materials and designs used by caddisflies in case-making may take many forms. Though you may not have realized it, the small pieces of wood and gravel sometimes found in the stomachs of trout and many other freshwater fish may be the remains of case-makers that have been eaten—cases and all.

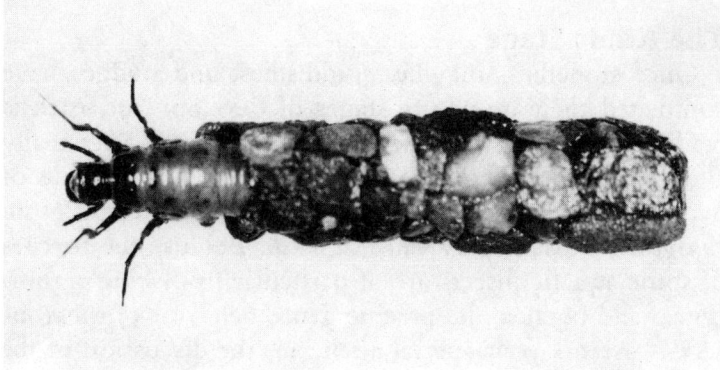

A "Portable" Caddisfly Habitat

The Pupal Stage

Of the major orders of aquatic insects we're considering, only caddisflies and midges have a pupal stage of development in their life cycles. The pupal stage is one in which the behavior of larvae in these orders and the physical changes they undergo are similar to those associated with the transformation of caterpillars into moths and butterflies.

A caddisfly case-maker generally prepares for its pupal stage by attaching its case to some underwater object and then sealing the case ends to form a kind of isolation chamber. It will remain in this chamber for several weeks prior to emerging. The prepupal stage preparations of "free living" caddisfly larvae (i.e., those that don't use portable habitats) are similar except that in the absence of a case, they secrete a silklike substance to form a protective shell that surrounds them during their pupal stage. [§13 and §14]

Like caddisflies, midge larvae complete their pupal stage within a pupal shell.

The Adult Stage

Once stoneflies, mayflies, caddisflies, and midges have completed their immature stages of development, each is ready to assume its flying form. This transition isn't really a developmental stage, it's a "happening," a miracle of nature. While some fly fishermen refer to the event as an *emergence,* most simply call it a *hatch.* Because the hatches of some aquatic insects are of particular fly-fishing significance, and because the preemergence behavior of these insects warrants your special attention, the discussion of the adult stage that follows begins with a brief comparison of insect activity levels in aquatic habitats immediately before and during a hatch.

Preparation for Emergence

If you were to observe a typical aquatic-insect habitat over a twenty-four-hour period, relatively little activity would be apparent during most daylight hours. The key word, though, is "apparent" because in the shadows provided by cover, nymphs and larvae of many species may be prowling about. In the afternoon, and especially as dusk approaches, activity in aquatic habitats increases. Yet even this activity level is limited when compared to that accompanying preparations for emergence; immature aquatic insects that have spent weeks, months, even years, in hiding seem to throw caution to the wind as they prepare to assume their flying forms. To illustrate, the nymphs of every species of stonefly and some mayflies will begin to migrate toward shallower water so they can climb out of it to hatch. Mayfly nymphs that must remain in water to emerge will begin swimming back and forth between bottom structure and the water's surface, or positioning themselves on the tops of submerged rocks or debris. Some will seek emergence sites on or near aquatic vegetation. Though hidden from direct view, caddisfly and midge larvae that have completed their pupal stage of development will begin freeing themselves from their isolation chambers or protective shells so they can float or propel themselves toward the water's surface to emerge. [§15] (Like some mayfly nymphs, the pupal forms of certain caddisflies emerge in water; others must leave it to hatch.)

Beyond these events, there are two more things you should remember about emergence activity. First, because some aquatic insects are nocturnal, their emergence will begin after nightfall. Second, because their actions occur in response to life cycles that may in previous generations have had hundreds of female insects laying thousands of eggs within minutes of one another, the number of immature aquatic insects preparing to hatch at essentially the same time may also be very large.

The Hatch

Witnessing a hatch is a memorable experience. Seeing aquatic insects that, until seconds before, may have been flat, greenish-colored nymphs, suddenly appear with delicate, brownish-gold bodies, long tails that seem to be made from strands of silk, and wings that quickly carry them away to meet others of their kind, isn't something that's easily forgotten.

It's a magical sight. One moment there's nothing on the water or in the air; the next, there's life. At first, newly emerged winged insects appear in ones and twos. Within seconds, however, there may be dozens. And if the hatch is a major one, within minutes, thousands may appear.

From an angling perspective, one of the most important things to remember about hatches is that some may be "simple" and involve only insects of a single species while others may be "complex" and involve the emergence of several species belonging to one or more orders.

As they emerge, stoneflies, caddisflies, and semi-adult mayflies usually have *two pairs* of functional wings; midges only have one.

A Mayfly Spinner

A Mayfly Dun

Having mentioned "wings," I can now address something you may have been wondering about since we began discussing aquatic insects. Whenever I've used the term *adult*, I've also usually mentioned *semi-adult*. That's because of mayflies. Look at these photographs of the same mayfly. The first was taken immediately after the mayfly's emergence; the second, approximately twenty-four hours later. As you can see, the wings of the first mayfly have a hazy, cloudy appearance. In the second, the wings have cleared. This difference arises because mayflies do something no other insect does—they molt, one final time, *after* they have the capacity to fly!

Fly fishermen have assigned names to the "before" and "after" final-molt phases of mayflies. Semi-adult mayflies that have just emerged and whose wings have a hazy or cloudy appearance are called *duns*. Mayflies that have completed their final molt and whose wings have cleared are called *spinners*. [§16] Only spinners are truly adult and thus capable of reproduction. (As we've discussed, stoneflies, caddisflies, and midges are sexually mature upon emergence.)

Just as time is an important consideration in terms of their life cycles, the same is true for the period needed by immature aquatic insects to hatch.

If you were to observe their emergence closely, you'd note that depending on order, species, and to some extent individuals, aquatic insects may require from a fraction of a second to several minutes to escape from their nymphal shucks or pupal shells and fly away. While time is of little concern to stoneflies that leave the water to emerge and are consequently inaccessible to feeding fish, for insects hatching in water it's a different story. For them, the time necessary to emerge may mean the difference between getting airborne and getting eaten.

It may take a mayfly emerging in water several minutes from the time it leaves cover as a nymph to reach the water's surface, struggle free from its nymphal shuck, and fly away as a dun. That struggle is one in which things can and do go wrong. And a careful inspection of mayfly emergence sites will usually reveal dead or dying specimens that fly fishermen sometimes refer to as "stillborns" or "cripples."

Even after successfully casting their nymphal shucks, mayflies emerging in water remain at risk until their wings dry and their flight muscles become functional. During this period they may often be seen floating defenseless on the water's surface. While carried along by currents, they often kick and twitch, inviting attacks by feeding fish. When weather conditions are marginal for emergence—for example, on very damp days—a dun may have to make several attempts to get airborne. And each time it "touches down" after failing to maintain flight, it offers fish another feeding opportunity.

Like mayflies, most caddisflies and midges struggle in the water to emerge. Under normal conditions, however, it takes them less time to leave the water after hatching than is the case for mayflies. In this regard, and unlike mayflies, adult caddisflies will often begin to run or flutter across the water's surface immediately after emerging.

Once they've taken flight, most of the aquatic insects we've been discussing will seek cover near streamside. It's while in such cover that the mayfly dun-to-spinner molt occurs.

Mating

Depending on species, adult aquatic insects may or may not feed or drink. All, however, will attempt to mate.

Given the variations in their life spans, it's hardly surprising that adult aquatic insects differ in their mating behavior. Some, like the midge, may begin mating within minutes after emerging. Those with longer life spans, such as stoneflies, may not mate for several days after hatching. Similarly, while aquatic insects like the mayfly mate only once, others like the caddisfly may mate several times.

In terms of mating locations, stoneflies and caddisflies usually mate on the ground, mayflies in the air, and midges wherever the opportunity presents itself.

Egg Laying

After mating, female aquatic insects will return to or near the water to lay eggs [§17]. The egg-laying methods used differ among insects within and between orders. However, an examination of the techniques illustrated will reveal something (of special fly-fishing importance) common to each of the methods shown. It's that females using any of the methods depicted will make themselves readily

accessible to hungry fish. Consequently, within hours after a hatch, the return of certain egg layers to the water—for example, female mayflies—may provide you with another opportunity to fish over very active "surface feeders."

A Spinner Fall

Unlike aquatic insects whose egg-laying females return to the water sporadically, the female spinners of certain mayfly species sometimes return in large numbers over a period of minutes. Fly fishermen refer to this event as a *spinner fall*.

Although spinner falls are sometimes seen in the morning, they're more often observed later in the day. In many regions, the probability of their occurrence increases toward dusk, with some beginning after nightfall. Given this variability, it's important whenever you're fishing or near the water to be on the alert for small groups of spinners whose flight paths have a characteristic up-and-down motion. If a major spinner fall is to occur, these early arrivals (usually males) will be joined by others, and mating or spinner clouds will form. While these clouds may be detected within a few feet of the water's surface, they're

Aquatic Insect Egg-Laying Methods

more often first seen at tree-top levels; fishermen who don't think to look *up* will miss them. Once formed, a spinner cloud will begin to settle slowly and female spinners that have entered the cloud will pull away, mate, and drop toward the water to start laying eggs.

During and after a spinner fall, egg layers often collapse on the water, spent from their efforts, and die. If this occurs subsequent to a major hatch, large numbers of *spent-wing* spinners (a term used in connection with some *down-wing* or *spread-wing* patterns) may be found blanketing the water's surface. And as is the case with a hatch, the sight of hundreds, sometimes thousands, of readily available and easily accessible insects floating in the water's surface film will often prompt fish to become very active surface feeders.

Shapes, Sizes, and Colors

Although shapes, sizes, and colors have been mentioned at several points in our discussion of aquatic insects, the significance of these factors in terms of pattern selection deserves elaboration.

If a pattern is described in terms of its length, width, and thickness, its size has effectively been established. While the same applies to insects, they do something patterns don't—they grow.

The sizes of some immature aquatic insects change while their outlines remain essentially the same. As a consequence, and from a pattern-selection perspective, it may be desirable to carry patterns that imitate insects like these in several sizes. Similarly, although adult insects don't grow, carrying patterns imitating them in different sizes may also be wise. Exercising this option may permit using a single pattern design to imitate insects of any number of orders and species where, though differing in size, their shapes and coloration are substantially the same.

Though practices differ, many fly fishermen studying angling entomology select or tie patterns whose sizes approximate the average size of the specimens of some species they've observed or collected. Many also make a point, however, of carrying patterns at least one, and sometimes two sizes *smaller* than average. This reflects a widely held belief that pattern *refusals*—that is, where fish move to a pattern but reject it at the last moment—often result from using a pattern that, though having the correct shape and color, is too large.

Fish can and do discriminate between colors. And immature and adult aquatic insects exhibit wide variations in coloration. Though the approach to matching insect and pattern colors generally follows that for shape and size—the closer the match, the better—there are some additional points regarding color that you should consider when making pattern selections.

The colors of the top and undersides of immature and adult aquatic insects often differ. Beyond these differences, some insects have prominent color features—for example, light or dark abdominal bands. For floating patterns, the bottom color of the insect a pattern represents will generally predominate. That's hardly surprising, considering fish approach such patterns from below. On the other hand, because fish can approach them from any angle to compare their appearance with the naturals they're accustomed to observing, underwater patterns may be tied with colors clearly differentiating between their tops and bottoms, and where appropriate, to show distinctive color features. Remember, when you're making pattern decisions, select colors on the basis of what a fish is most apt to see, not those you'll likely observe if you simply hold an insect in your hand and look at it from above.

Behavior

While applying "appearance" data in making pattern selections will certainly increase your chance of success, using insect behavioral data in conjunction with the *right* pattern will almost guarantee that you'll catch more, bigger, or smarter fish.

In years past, the term *presentation* was often interpreted to mean only the manner in which a pattern was delivered—that is, casting a traditional dry fly so that it would land lightly on the water's surface. More recently, however, the term has come to mean both a pattern's delivery and its movement once on or in the water. The angling implication of this redefinition isn't something you can afford to overlook because the relationship between insect behavior and pattern presentation is extremely important.

Beyond case-making, constructing nets with which to capture food and using tethers to position themselves in flowing currents, immature aquatic insects exhibit a variety of other behaviors. While you'll enjoy investigating them as you continue studying angling entomology, a behavior that's of more immediate, practical angling importance concerns the different methods aquatic nymphs and larvae use to move about in their watery worlds.

Immature aquatic insects usually transport themselves by either crawling or swimming. While most are slow crawlers, some can move rapidly. Similarly, while many nymphs are awkward swimmers, a few are not. And quite apart from any preferred "normal" method of travel, when separated from their habitats and carried along by water currents, many immature aquatic insects simply *dead drift,* exhibiting no independent movement.

Like the methods used by their immature forms to transport themselves, the flight characteristics of stoneflies, mayflies, caddisflies, and midges vary.

Stoneflies, especially the larger ones, are relatively slow

fliers. They appear to be underpowered and, as a consequence, seem to have trouble maneuvering. Stoneflies generally travel in more or less straight lines. And in the case of a large stonefly, the beat of its two pairs of wings can easily be seen.

Mayflies are relatively slow but steady fliers. While airborne, they may often be seen almost to stop their forward motion, drop several inches, and then continue on their way. Unlike the labored flight of stoneflies, mayflies seem to fly effortlessly.

Caddisflies are excellent fliers. They have the power and balance necessary to move quickly and change directions without difficulty. Their relatively small size, combined with these flight characteristics, generally makes it easy to differentiate flying caddisflies from stoneflies or mayflies.

The most obvious airborne characteristic of midges is their erratic flight path. Like mosquitoes, they circle, dive, and rise without apparent purpose. And like mosquitoes, they tend to fly in clouds with others of their kind.

The different methods of transport used by aquatic insects in their immature and flying forms have significant angling implications insofar as insect recognition and pattern presentation are concerned. As a consequence, one of your early insect-collecting objectives should be to determine which particular movement-related behaviors apply to the specific insects you've decided to study. This won't be as difficult as you might imagine because insects of a particular species will usually transport themselves and react to being transported by water in some characteristic manner.

Combining Facts and Applying Conclusions

In "Getting Started" I indicated that as you gather facts you should ask yourself, "Is this information I can use in connection with other data I've collected?" The following will illustrate both the importance of that point and the kind of informational relationships you should look for as you continue your study effort.

We've just finished separately addressing two subjects—aquatic insect "shapes, sizes, and colors" and "behavior." While each of these characteristics is important in its own right, their true angling significance can better be seen if they're considered *together*.

Like humans, fish develop associations between things. When you turn the ignition on in your automobile, you expect the engine to start. For its part, when a fish observes an insect it's accustomed to seeing, it expects the insect both to appear and to behave naturally. Obviously, then, the probability of getting a fish to take a pattern increases when that pattern's appearance *and* behavior duplicate those of the insect it imitates. Affecting this "match" requires:

1. that a pattern's shape, size, and color closely resemble those of its insect counterpart;
2. a pattern be cast so that its arrival at a fish's holding position or "lie" will appear as expected; and,
3. once in or on the water and in a position where it can be seen by a fish, a pattern be manipulated in a manner that will cause it to act like the insect it's intended to represent. Given that during a major hatch, fish like trout may become *selective* feeders and only take insects of a specific form and species no matter how many other insects may be accessible simultaneously, it's almost impossible to overstate the importance of matching pattern selections and presentations to the shapes, sizes, colors, and behavior of the insects on which you think fish may be feeding.

This is also true even when there is no hatch to match.

TERRESTRIAL INSECTS

Consider: many more insect species develop on land than in water; their habitats may be found almost anywhere; and, depending on species, their peak emergence activity may frequently occur after that of most aquatic insects of major concern to fly fishermen. Given this, you'd think anglers interested in extending their season would be especially anxious to learn more about terrestrials. Not so. Many believe terrestrials are of little or no importance.

Several factors have acted to downgrade the significance of terrestrials in the minds of fly fishermen.

- The bulk of fly-fishing literature focuses on aquatic insects.
- Many fly fishermen only schedule trips for periods during which hatches or spinner falls are anticipated.
- Many fly fishermen imagine terrestrials are only rarely accessible to fish.

While aquatic insects are of greater fly-fishing significance, terrestrials are an important food source for many freshwater fish. Indeed, in some areas and during some parts of the year—such as late spring through the summer—ants, beetles, grasshoppers, and other terrestrials are typically the insect forms that trout and other freshwater fish most often expect to see.

Availability and Accessibility

There's no need to worry about the availability of terrestrials. They can be found by the hundreds near all the waters you fish. Their accessibility, however, is something that needs to be examined more closely because contrary to general belief, and notwithstanding that they usually enter the water by accident, *terrestrials are frequently accessible to fish.*

A wide variety of accidents attributable to man and nature result in terrestrials entering the water.

- Mowing fields or clearing brush may catapult terrestrials into water inhabited by fish.
- The construction of bridges or other structures may excavate terrestrials and deposit them in nearby water.
- Fly fishermen may knock terrestrials into the water by brushing against streamside foliage.
- Strong winds or even light breezes may deposit small terrestrials in the water.
- Run-offs from rain frequently carry terrestrials to fish.
- Winged terrestrials often crashland in water.

Considering the frequency with which these and similar events occur and the large numbers of terrestrials available, the belief that land insects are only rarely accessible to fish is clearly a misconception.

Life Cycles and Developmental Stages

Terrestrials have life cycles similar to those of aquatic insects. Like their aquatic cousins, all terrestrials have egg, nymphal or larval, and adult developmental stages. Only some, however, have a pupal stage.

The Egg Stage

As with aquatic insects, the egg stage of immature terrestrial development is of no angling consequence to those interested only in the fundamentals of angling entomology.

The Nymphal or Larval Stage

The wide variations in shape, size, and color associated with aquatic nymphs and larvae are also exhibited by immature terrestrials. Unlike their aquatic counterparts, however, terrestrial insects in their nymphal or larval stages are not continuously available to feeding fish. Those most frequently accessible either develop in habitats found in ground, foliage, or decaying organic matter located near water, or have the capacity to transport themselves to or near the water.

The Pupal Stage

Terrestrials in this stage of development undergo the same kinds of major changes in appearance as do aquatic insects. However, unlike aquatic insects, terrestrials in their pupal stage are of limited interest to fly fishermen. Indeed, except for major environmental disruptions, or some unusual event like a hornet's nest falling into the water, significant numbers of terrestrials in their pupal forms are rarely found in the water.

Emergence and the Adult Stage

While large numbers of terrestrials may emerge over short periods of time and adults may form clouds or swarms, in most regions this behavior doesn't have the special angling significance of an aquatic insect hatch.

Shapes, Sizes, and Colors

The shapes, sizes, and colors of immature and adult terrestrials are certainly important. And the matching concept discussed in connection with aquatic insects also applies to terrestrial pattern selection. The bent legs of the grasshopper and the color of a particular species (which varies greatly); the two globes on the ant; the oval shape of the beetle—all these should be observed and imitated with great care.

Behavior

Of the things that can alert fish to the presence of "insects that develop on land," the sounds produced by terrestrials when they come in contact with the water are of particular importance.

The sounds you and I hear are generated by the movement of air. If that movement has a familiar pattern, we associate the sound with something, such as a friendly voice or an alarm bell. The sounds fish "hear" are generated by the movement of water. They sense this movement through membrane-covered ears on the sides of their heads and special nerve endings located along the length of their bodies.

As with humans, fish associate meanings with the sounds they hear. For example, sounds produced by a noisy wader signal danger and will drive fish away from the sound's source. On the other hand, sounds produced by insects struggling in water often attract fish. If you apply this hearing concept to fly fishing, it should be clear that the sound, or absence of it, associated with a terrestrial pattern entering the water will be an important factor in shaping a fish's response to the pattern's presence. And if the sound waves produced after its entry into the water imitate those which fish associate with terrestrials that have become "accessible," you can almost bet that pattern will get some attention. Anglers applying the basics of angling entomology can deliver a terrestrial pattern like a black beetle so that it will make a noisy entry into the water to imitate the sound of a beetle crash-landing; then they manipulate the pattern to simulate the reaction of a black beetle that's found itself in a foreign environment. (Obviously, the presentation of a large grasshopper or an ant would differ from that of a black beetle or, for that matter, from one another.)

Depending on order, species, and to some extent individuals, terrestrials react differently when they find themselves in water. Some:

- Don't move at all.
- Kick and flutter momentarily, stop all movement, and then, seconds later, repeat these actions.
- Attempt to swim by kicking their legs or paddling with their wings.

It's important to remember that to the extent terrestrials move once in the water, they reveal themselves to be living creatures as opposed to inanimate objects; they generate sounds that permit fish to define their location. Consequently, it's essential that you make a special point of observing and noting both the differing ways in which terrestrials enter the water and their various "post-accident" behaviors. Without such information, it will be difficult for you to make informed decisions regarding terrestrial pattern presentations.

INSECT IDENTIFICATION

Whether examining insect photographs or specimens collected in the field, you're soon going to find yourself asking, "What is it?" Learning to recognize and identify specific insects is thus another very important part of angling entomology.

Precision

Insects can be identified with varying degrees of precision. For example, imagine that you show me an adult insect which, while at rest, holds its wings in a vertical position above its body and ask, "What is it?" I could respond by answering:

- "It's a mayfly (an insect of a particular *order*)."
- "It's a mayfly (and cite a particular *family*)."
- "It's a mayfly (and cite a particular family and *genus*)."
- "It's a mayfly (and cite a particular family, genus, and *species*)."

(In the sequence shown, the terms *order, family, genus,* and *species* denote progressively more precise levels of insect identification. [§18])

The degree of precision needed in insect identification is dictated by communication requirements. The more you communicate with others, the more important precision becomes. To illustrate, if you've just started to study angling entomology and want chiefly to record data for your own use, your need for precision in insect identification will be limited. However, because anglers studying at an intermediate level tend to communicate more with others and use different references, precision will be of greater concern. For fly fishermen studying at advanced levels, the need for precise insect identification—that is, being able to specify the order, family, genus, and species of an insect—will be the norm.

Even though the need for precision in insect identification will be limited early in your study efforts, you're still going to have to adopt some method of telling one insect apart from another. Reason? Because when you begin collecting insects and recording data, you're going to find many insects in the *same* order and developmental stage

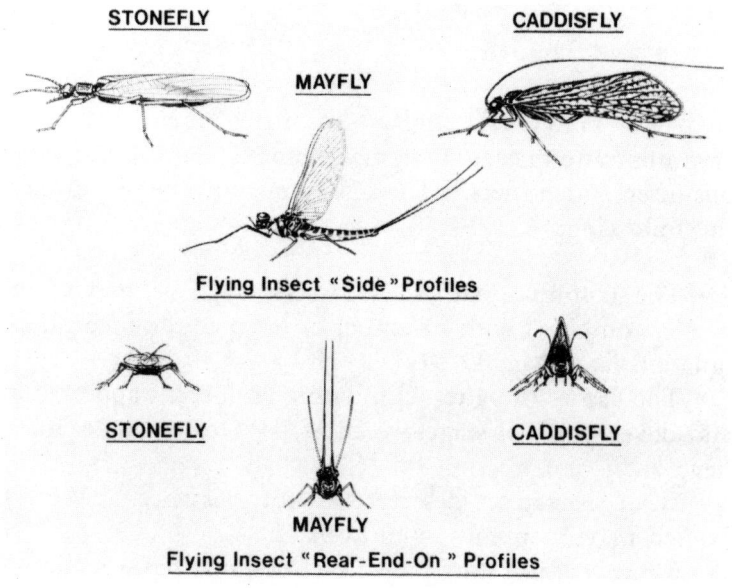

Flying Insect "Side" Profiles

Flying Insect "Rear-End-On" Profiles

"At Rest" Wing Positions

but exhibiting very *different* physical and behavioral characteristics. Remember the importance of knowing which specific insects inhabit the water *you* fish, when *you* fish; remember the modifying effects of life cycles on insect forms, sizes, shapes, colors, and behaviors; and remember the relationship of these factors to pattern selections and presentations. From this, it should be clear that for record keeping and other purposes, you'll need to use some method of insect identification just to communicate with yourself, let alone anyone else. A question that naturally arises is, If identifying insects by order and form isn't always sufficient, but identifying them precisely isn't always necessary either, what's the alternative?

The Informal Method

Many fly fishermen beginning the study of angling entomology use informal methods of insect identification to differentiate between insects of the same or different orders, species, and forms. These informal methods are created by individual anglers to meet their particular communication needs. Informal methods make use of various insect "identifiers." These may include one or more of the following:

- The common names of insects, such as mayfly or beetle, combined with a number or letter to produce a designation like "Mayfly #6."
- The names of patterns imitating an insect's appearance and developmental stage—such as, a "Green Drake Spinner."
- Brief narrative descriptors—for instance, "White-bodied mayfly spinner, #10 hook."
- Some combination of these designations—such as, "Green Drake, mayfly spinner #6, #10 hook."

Whatever its form, an identifier assigned an insect is one which, to the individual doing the assigning, represents some set of specific physical characteristics—for example, a greenish-brown nymph approximately 8 mm in length. Unfortunately, identifiers used by one angler won't usually bring to mind the same set of specifics to anyone else or be employed for insect identification purposes in more advanced references.

The problems generated by using informal methods of insect identification have long been recognized. Some of these are

- The confusion generated by using different names to identify a single insect, or attempting to identify insects solely on the basis of their general appearance.
- The difficulties encountered by fly fishermen in different regions attempting to discuss specific insects inhabiting the water they fish.
- The inability of fly fishermen to locate information in

references applicable to a particular insect in the absence of knowing the insect's scientific name.
• The frustration resulting when fly fishermen, attempting to analyze and apply their own data, forget the specific meanings of the informal identifiers they've created!

To eliminate, or at least minimize, these and other insect identification problems and to improve their ability to communicate, all fly fisherman studying angling entomology at advanced levels, and many interested only in basics, have adopted the formal or scientific method of insect identification.

The Formal Method

In simplest terms, the formal method of insect identification involves examining an insect or "natural" and comparing its structural features (as opposed to general appearance) with those of different insects described in special references. The objective of the comparison is to find a "match." Users of the formal method are guided in the comparison process by narrative or illustrative "keys." In effect, a key asks a user to examine a particular structural feature on a natural, to compare the observed feature with two options described in the key, and to select the best match. Initially, the matching process involves comparing obvious structural features such as the presence or absence of wing pads. As the process continues, however, progressively finer levels of structural detail are compared, such as the relationship between the lengths of leg segments. With each successive match, the degree of precision increases. When it's been established that all the structural features of a natural are identical to those of some insect described in a key extending down to the level of species, the key will provide the insect's scientific name. That

An Illustrated Narrative Key

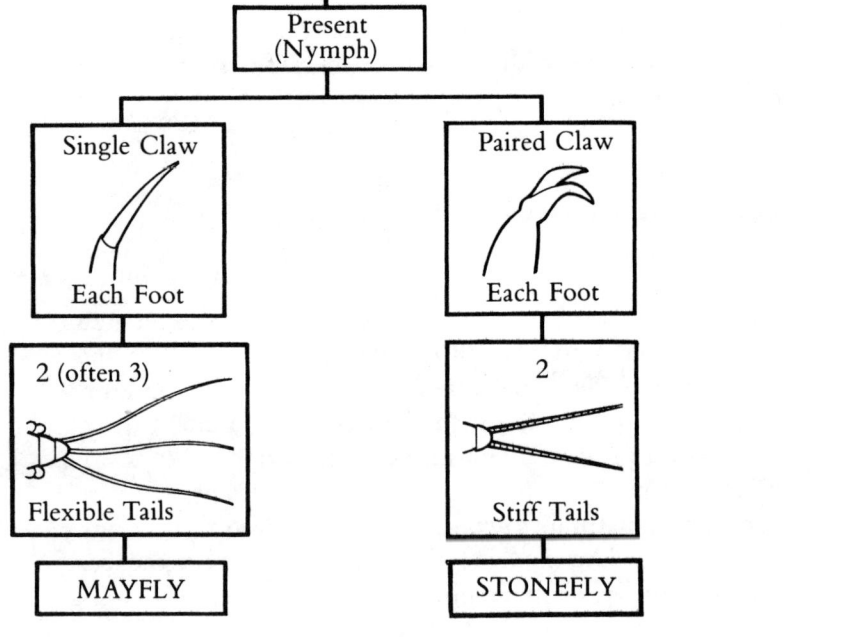

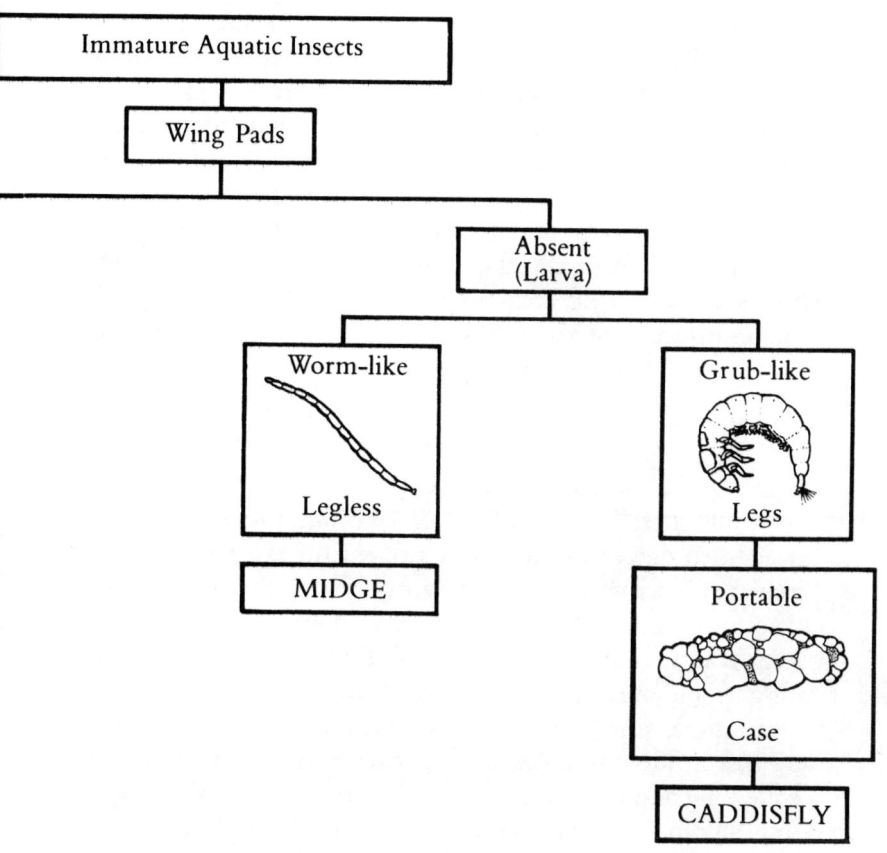

name, composed of the insect's genus and species, will be in Latin. [§19]

While learning to use keys takes some practice, employing the formal method of insect identification has many advantages over any informal method. It makes use of standardized terminology; it may be used to identify insects to the varying degrees of precision required to meet differing communications needs; it produces a unique name that differentiates a particular insect (and all those *identical* to it) from all other insects; and, finally, it permits fly fishermen in different regions to communicate regarding an insect with a high probability that they're both talking about the same insect.

Which Method Should I Try?

While there's no doubt that learning to use the keys needed to determine an insect's scientific name will, in the long run, prove more than worth the effort, it's equally true that using informal insect identifiers can carry you a long way toward achieving the objective of catching more, bigger, and smarter fish. In this regard, and recognizing its limitations, don't hesitate to employ an informal method of insect identification in support of your early insect-collecting and data-recording activities. Once you've begun to use your data and have satisfied yourself that applying an understanding of insect forms and behavior has made you a more successful fly fisherman, and once you've experienced some of the problems that arise from using informal methods of insect identification, you'll have the motivation needed to learn and apply the formal method. When you begin to use it, remember:

• If the opportunity exists, have someone familiar with the formal method "walk you through" its application using insects *you've* collected. This approach will permit you to ask questions as you begin using keys and produce an end product—that is, insect identifications—relevant to your study effort.

- Let your communication needs determine the degree of precision toward which you strive. Focus your early attempts at insect identification and the use of keys to assign insects to their proper orders and families. Don't worry about identifying them precisely if that degree of precision isn't required to meet a real communication requirement.
- As you begin dealing with Latin terms, concentrate on recognizing their printed or written forms. You're going to see them more often than you'll hear them. Don't be embarrassed if your pronunciation of Latin terms differs from that of someone else. Yours may be correct!
- Once you've identified some insects and are confident of the accuracy of your determinations, go back and update the data you've previously recorded by inserting the scientific names of the insects you've collected. This will substantially increase the future usefulness of your "old" data.

While it's essential to learn about the forms and behaviors of insects in or near the water you fish, the habitats in which they're found and develop, and how to identify them, the *fun* of studying angling entomology really starts when you begin collecting insects in the field.

The equipment and procedures needed to do that are our next topics for discussion.

3

Collecting, Rearing, and Preserving Insects

Collecting insects and other material in the field is the principal means by which the data needed to make informed pattern selection and presentation decisions are obtained. While collecting doesn't require sophisticated equipment or procedures, it does demand some thought if you want to get quick, positive results.

WHERE SHOULD I COLLECT?
Your initial collecting activities should focus on developing a working knowledge of the insect habitat and

population distributions to be found in or near the water *you* most frequently fish. In terms of specifics, there are three things you should remember insofar as "where" is concerned.

First, when you're ready to begin collecting from a section of water, mentally divide the site to be investigated into segments. (A 300-yard stretch of a typical mountain trout stream might be divided into three 100-yard segments.) Having done this, select several specific sites for sampling that have the same apparent physical characteristics (for example, three or four different riffles) and are distributed over the length of the segment. Repeat this same procedure for the other major habitat-types to be found along the segment (such as collections of large rocks, submerged debris, and the like). The product of applying this method of habitat-type site selection might look like the distribution shown for the stream segment illustrated.

While this site selection method won't provide a detailed picture of the insect habitat and population distributions associated with a piece of water, it *will* provide a feel for the general nature of those distributions. And in terms of quickly getting about the business of catching fish, having a general feel that can be applied in making pattern selection and presentation decisions *over the entire length of a segment* is better than having a detailed knowledge that applies to only one or two locations in the segment.

Second, and with regard to the actual collection of insects, because some of their immature forms leave the water to emerge, and after hatching, almost all of the aquatic insects we've been discussing are able to fly, *immature, semi-adult,* and *adult aquatic insects* should be collected wherever found—in, on, or near the water you fish.

Finally, because those of major interest to fly fishermen tend to be accident prone, *immature and adult terrestrials*

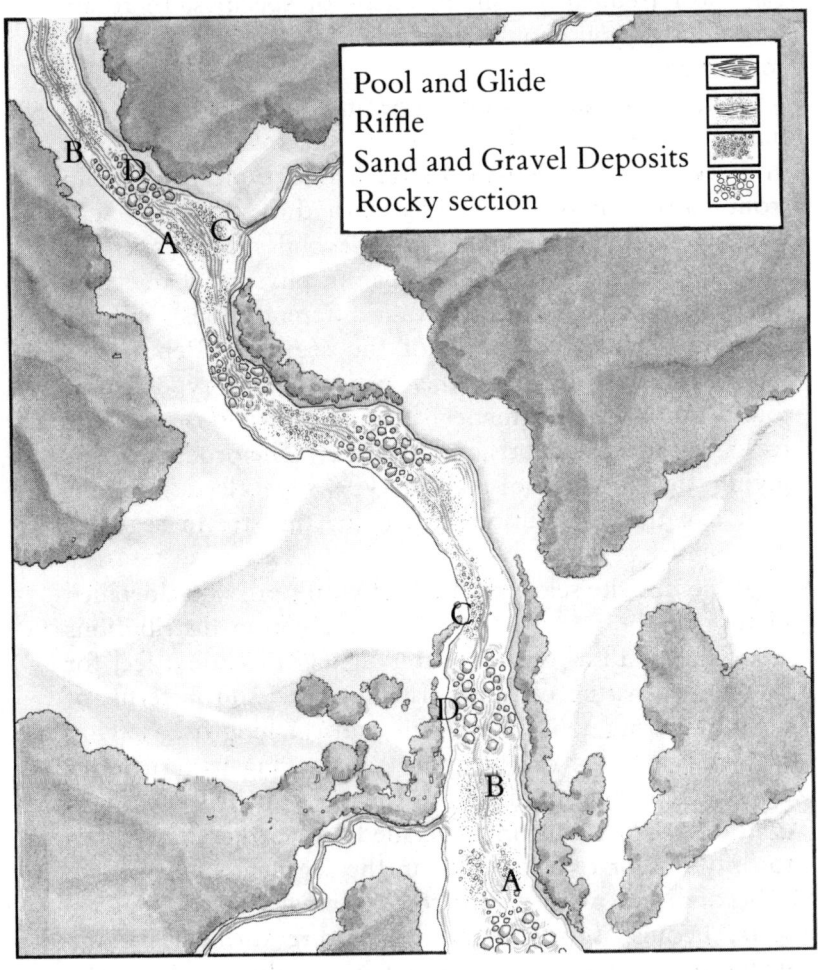

Collection Site Distribution

Collecting, Rearing, and Preserving Insects

should be collected wherever found in or on the water, or in any transitional zones adjacent to the water you fish.

WHEN SHOULD I COLLECT?

The time to begin collecting is after you reach the general area in which you intend to fish, but *before* you begin implementing your site selection/sampling strategy. And the thing to do is simply to spend some time looking around. As you do, make a special point to:

- Inspect the surfaces of structures, trees, and rocks near the water for resting adults, discarded shucks, or other clues indicating the presence of insect populations.
- Look in pools and along the edge of the water for evidence of immature aquatic insect preemergence activity.
- Check for flying insects leaving or returning to the water.
- Look for feeding fish.

A variety of very important angling-related observations can be made while just "looking around." For example, your arrival in an area may have coincided with the beginning of a hatch; observing a mating cloud may indicate a spinner fall is imminent, or investigating fish feeding against a river bank may reveal a source of some accident-prone terrestrials. Since events of these kinds are difficult to predict, you must be prepared to adjust your collecting and fishing plans quickly to take advantage of their occurrence. Remember, begin collecting by using your powers of observation.

Given that you'll be collecting to obtain data describing the physical and behavioral characteristics of insects found in or near the water you fish, when you fish, it's only logical that it's when you plan to fish that you should initially plan to collect. However, once you've finished collecting in an area, it's important to remain alert for conditions arising that may signal the need to restudy that area. Some specific conditions include:

• Sustained changes in the volume, flow rates, temperature, or quality of the water you fish.
• Extreme and sustained changes in climatic conditions in areas containing water you fish.
• Changes in your normal fishing routine or schedule. (Remember, in the context of insect life cycles, a shift of a few days at certain times of the year can make a big difference in the insect species and forms found in an area.)
• An ability to employ new fishing methods.

Another important point to consider in connection with "when" relates to establishing the sequence in which running-water habitats are to be sampled. When you've selected the specific habitats in a brook, stream, or river to be sampled, make sure their sampling sequence has you working in an *upstream* direction. Beyond the obvious advantage that by working upstream, insects suspended in water will be carried into your collector, an added advantage is that sediments or other debris disturbed by your collecting activities will remain behind you and not cloud the site you're examining.

The last point that should be mentioned concerning "when" involves a mistake made by many fly fishermen who've just begun to collect. While it's essential to be alert for opportunities to collect wherever and whenever you're near or on the water, don't attempt to fish and steadily collect. This is *not* to say that you should only collect or fish on any given trip. A better approach is simply to set aside some time on each trip when you can concentrate on collecting. While you may be concerned this will interfere

Collecting, Rearing, and Preserving Insects

with fishing, it's unlikely you'll find it a problem. Indeed, once you've begun experiencing the thrill of discovery that accompanies collecting insects, the reverse is more apt to be the case.

HOW SHOULD I COLLECT?

Insects of interest to fly fishermen are collected in many ways. Consequently, any specific answer to "how" will depend on the insect species and forms you've decided to collect, the nature and location of the habitats from which you'll be collecting, and the collecting equipment you've chosen to employ.

Equipment

Some of the pieces of equipment that can be used to collect insects include garden trowels, small rakes, hoes, and wooden probes to dislodge insects from their habitats, and nets and seines of various sizes to capture them.

Some items commonly used in support of insect-collecting activities include containers and cages, tweezers, rulers, pocket magnifying glasses, and pin probes to house, transport, and examine specimens, and notebooks, logs, or special data sheets to record essential data.

Once you've begun collecting insects, you'll quickly find that, beyond the equipment and items I've listed, there are dozens of other gadgets and devices to be found on the market and elsewhere that can be very useful for collecting and related purposes in the field and at home. Many of these will be listed in catalogs distributed by biological supply houses. Others will be found on the shelves of local stores. Some will be adaptations of things intended for other purposes. To illustrate:

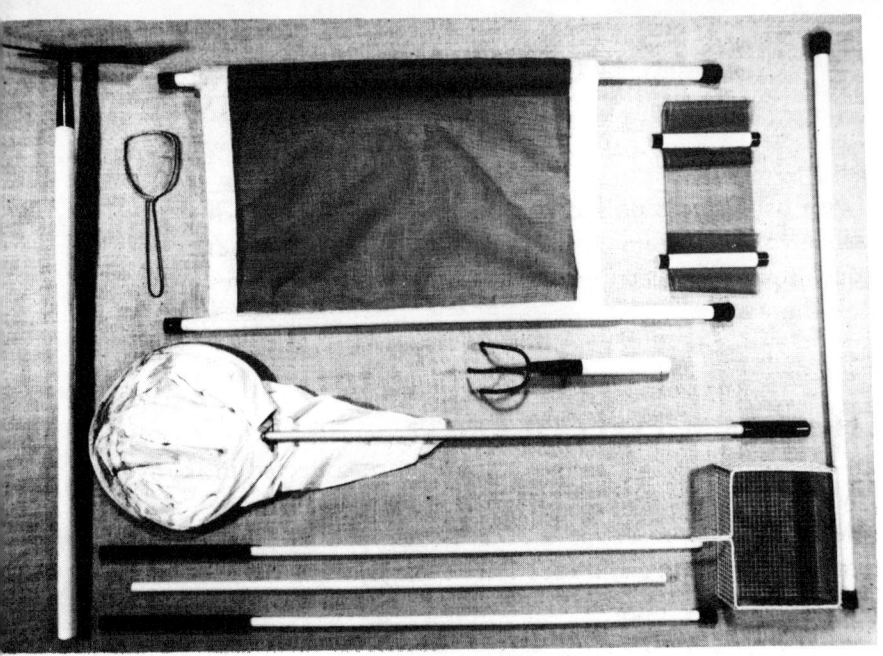

Dislodgers and Collectors

• Pill-box-size plastic cosmetic containers that can be carried in a trouser pocket make transporting or storing both aquatic and terrestrial insects easy.

• Small plastic devices are available into which an insect can be placed and then inspected under a built-in magnifying lens.

• Large, one-gallon plastic jugs that are ideal for transporting immature aquatic insects can often be obtained free of charge from "fast food" outlets.

• The plastic plates found in some microwave dinner packages can be used to hold aquatic nymphs, larvae, and the like while they're being separated for inspection or storage.

• Hard-bodied insects can be stored in plastic, twist-lock cap "prescription" bottles.

• When carried in a fishing-vest pocket, the thin-walled, threaded-cap, plastic vials used by coin collectors can be used to capture and temporarily store insects.

Not all of the items shown in the accompanying photographs, or that you may otherwise accumulate, will be needed every time you collect. The specific pieces required will be determined by what and where you're collecting. Similarly, although most of the collecting equipment you'll need can be purchased, much of it can often be found around your house or easily and inexpensively built.

Procedures

While the procedures used to collect insects vary according to the forms to be captured and the characteristics of the habitats to be sampled, some insect collecting techniques that can easily be used by fly fishermen include the following.

In running water, a piece of fiberglass window screening stretched between two poles to form a large seine can be used to collect most immature aquatic insects. To collect in undisturbed water, the seine is simply lowered so that insects in or on the water are carried to it. If insects inhabiting bottom structure are to be collected, a short-handled garden rake or hoe can be used to agitate rocks, debris, and sediment deposits upstream from the seine so that insects dislodged from these habitats are carried to it. A variation on this collecting technique involves using an aquarium dip net or a small, narrow piece of window screening attached to two short handles (a small seine) that can be carried in your fishing vest or pocket. Collectors like these can be used to capture insects floating by while you're fishing, or to sample quiet eddies or gentle surface currents.

Collecting beyond arm's length in deep or still water often requires equipment of special design and construction. For example, the handles of collectors used for this purpose may be segmented so their lengths may be adjusted. And the collector areas on these extended-handle

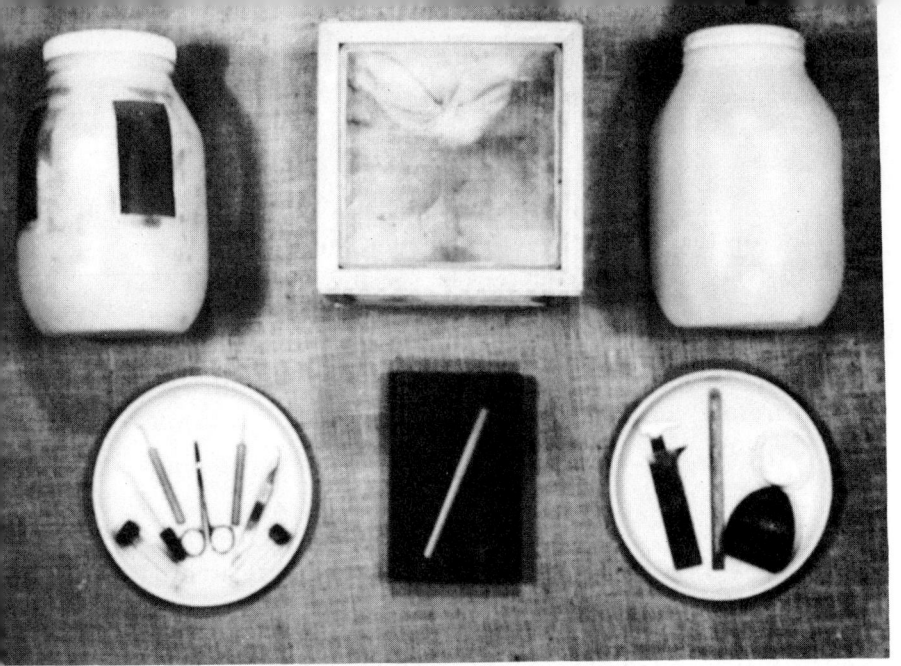

Containers and Miscellaneous Equipment

seines are typically reinforced with wire screening to prevent their collapse when used to dislodge insects from vegetative or deep-water habitats.

Tweezers are used to lift insects from collector screens so that they can be examined or placed in transport containers. Examinations may be performed in the field so that data regarding insect size, shape, and color may immediately be applied in making pattern selection and presentation decisions, or insects may, instead, be taken home for later and more careful study.

When immature aquatic insects must be transported from one collection site to another, an open container can be used. An open container is simply a widemouthed, plastic jug with windows cut in its sides and lid. These windows (covered with plastic screening) are located in the upper two-thirds of the container so that when it's immersed, air can escape from the container and water can enter and circulate. This circulation will provide insects inside the container with the supply of new water and dissolved oxygen needed to keep them fresh and alive. The

Using a Large Seine and Hoe

absence of windows in the bottom third of the container will permit some water to remain in it after it's lifted from a stream or pool. This water will serve as a mobile habitat for insects being carried from one collecting site to another.

There are two things to remember when using open containers. First, containers of this type should be lifted from the water slowly and carefully to permit water in the upper two-thirds of the container to escape gradually. This will both allow time for insects inside the container to settle toward the bottom without damaging themselves and prevent water from splashing on you as you carry the container about. Second, containers carrying insects should not be shaken any more than necessary. Water sloshing inside can easily damage insects. Putting some dead leaves or aquatic vegetation in the container so that insects can attach themselves to it for stability and protection will reduce the probability of such damage.

From a spectator's viewpoint, it would be hard to imagine anything funnier than the sight of a fly fisherman "decked out" to fish, thrashing about with a fly rod in one hand and a butterfly net in the other, trying to capture a little dun that no one else can see. In practice, however, collecting flying insects rarely produces this kind of show.

A butterfly net usually serves as the primary collector for flying insects. While everyone's seen a butterfly net used for this purpose, this device may also be used in some not-so-common ways. For example, a small tree branch may be inserted into a net bag so that when the branch is shaken, insects clinging to it will fall into the bag. A butterfly net may also be swept through foliage to capture any winged aquatic or terrestrial insects.

While using a butterfly net to collect insects is simple, remember to rotate the net handle more than 90° after capturing an insect so that the collecting bag folds back on itself. This will close the bag while you continue looking for other insects or until you're ready to transfer those already captured into a holding cage.

An Open Transport Container

Many flying insects you may want to collect will be found resting on the surface of some object. These can often be captured simply by placing a small container over them and then, while the container is pressed lightly against the surface on which the insect is resting, slowly and carefully edging the container forward until it touches the insect. When they're touched, most insects will fly toward the closed end of the container. By lifting the container and quickly covering its open end with your thumb or the container's lid, the capture can be completed. As long as you continue carrying the covered container *upside down,* insects inside will tend to stay at its closed end. Because of this characteristic behavior, it is often possible to collect many insects in a single container quickly.

Once collected, flying insects, like others, may be examined and released, or placed in cages of various designs for transport or safekeeping. Some cages are constructed with wire-screen sides that provide flying insects with a surface they can grasp to steady themselves when the cage is moved, and a dry-air environment that will permit some to continue their development.

Perhaps the most basic insect datacollecting technique is the one illustrated. It simply involves noting the sizes, shapes, and colors of immature aquatic insects found clinging to the surface of a rock or piece of debris lifted from the water. While "reading" rocks won't provide information describing the full extent of the aquatic insect populations inhabiting a site, it will usually provide an indication of whether there is any insect activity at all. And identifying water that's barren of insect life is an important finding because that water is much less deserving of your angling time than water containing insect populations that will tend to attract and hold fish.

There's one last point I want to emphasize in connection

The Most Basic Insect Collecting Technique

with collecting before moving on to our next subject. Collecting insects isn't dangerous *if you're careful*. In this regard, don't collect in running water where water depths, or flow rates can create problems. Don't move about in still water unless you're absolutely sure of your footing. And don't become so preoccupied watching an insect's flight path that you forget to watch your own footing.

REARING INSECTS

While collecting insects is an essential part of studying angling entomology, rearing them *isn't*. But "growing your own" takes little time, effort, and equipment and can be a lot of fun. Like many others who have begun studying angling entomology, you may wish to try it. So, let's briefly discuss what rearing insects involves.

Creating a Home Habitat

The first task in preparing to rear insects is to select an

area at home in which to locate your insect project. If available, the area should be one in which there's a sink and source of tap water to facilitate cleaning equipment; there should also be an electrical outlet, and either natural light or light that can be available for daylong periods. It should *not* be an area in a main traffic pattern or one frequently used in support of routine household activities.

Your next task will be to assemble a "home habitat." These habitats typically consist of some kind of container, rocks and other materials to be placed in the container, water, and a screen cover. Home habitat designs can vary markedly. The first one shown is of simple construction. It consists simply of a shallow plastic pan, several rocks, sand and gravel, water, a few dead leaves, and a food-net container cover. The habitat design shown in the second photograph is more elaborate. It makes use of a twenty-gallon aquarium tank. Beyond the materials placed in the tank to create a typical mountain stream-like habitat, this particular design incorporates a life-support system. The

A Simple Home Habitat Design

A More Elaborate Home Habitat Design

small, inexpensive aerator and airstone bubbling system shown will oxygenate water in the aquarium and provide some water circulation from bubble action. Note the sand and gravel gradient in the bottom of the aquarium. It provides for varying water depths and facilitates the escape of immature aquatic insect forms that must emerge out of water. The larger sticks and rocks shown in the habitat have been positioned to extend above its waterline for the same purpose.

Water is obviously an essential component of any home habitat. And water taken from sites at which the insects you intend to rear were collected is the best to use. Because they will be accustomed to its quality and temperature, using this water will minimize the shock insects experience when being relocated from their home to yours. (Bringing home five gallons of extra water in a plastic container when you collect your insects will provide the supply needed to activate your home habitat and for its subsequent maintenance. Extra water should be stored in a cool, dark place.)

Selecting Insects

While it's technically possible to rear insects of almost any species, focus your first attempts at rearing insects on immature aquatic insects collected from water you regularly fish. Until you've gained some experience in preparing and maintaining a home habitat, you'll probably have the greatest success beginning with some of the larger stonefly and nonburrowing mayfly nymphs. If you decide to rear nymphs in these orders, try to select those having swollen or darkened wing pads. By selecting specimens with these characteristics, the probability of having some insects hatch shortly after activating your home habitat will be greatly increased. If rearing stoneflies and mayflies is inconsistent with your personalized selection of insects, then try a "mixed bag" including some case-makers and other nymphal, larval, or pupal forms, and see what happens. Experimenting adds to the excitement and fun of growing your own.

Collecting and Transporting Insects

Insects to be reared at home can, of course, be collected and transported using the procedures we've just discussed. There is, however, one additional thing I should mention. If it will take more than an hour to transport the insects you intend to rear home from the site where they were captured, consider putting the container in which your insects are being transported into an inexpensive Styrofoam cooler-chest partially filled with stream water. This will minimize water-temperature changes. You may also wish to consider using a flashlight battery-powered aerator to oxygenate water in the container during the trip home.

Activating a Home Habitat

All that's required to activate a home habitat is to: (1) add water to a level one to two inches above the highpoint of any sand and gravel gradient; (2) turn on any life-support systems you're using; (3) assure yourself that your insects are alive and not badly damaged; (4) transfer those to be reared into the habitat; and (5) cover the habitat. *Don't forget step 5.*

Maintaining a Home Habitat

Regardless of the insects you've decided to rear, maintaining a home habitat will require the use of natural or artificial light to illuminate the habitat during daylight hours, the periodic addition of water to compensate for evaporation and, if life-support systems are used, the daily monitoring of their operation.

Depending on species, and the length of time they're in your home habitat, it may also be necessary to feed the insects you've chosen to rear.

Aquatic insects have varied appetites. Some feed on vegetable matter, others on other insects. There are several sources of insect food you can use. One or two large dead leaves added to the habitat once a week or so will meet the food needs of many caddisfly larvae and some stonefly nymphs. The decomposition of these leaves will, in turn, provide food for other immature caddisflies, mayflies, and midges. Adding a few free-living caddisfly larvae or mayfly nymphs will satisfy the food requirements of any predators you've chosen to rear. [§20 and §21]

Testing Your Patience

The most difficult part of rearing insects is waiting for some-

thing to happen.

After activating your home habitat, inspect it carefully every morning and evening. Make a special point of examining the rocks and sticks extending above the water's surface. If you're lucky, one of these inspections will reveal an insect in transition from its nymphal or pupal to flying form. Take time to observe this event in its entirety. It's not often you'll have a chance to see a miracle. What you'll ordinarily find, however, will be discarded nymphal shucks, and winged insects clinging to the underside of the habitat's screen cover.

If several weeks after activating your home habitat you haven't had any insects hatch and don't see any moving about, there are two things you can do to determine if all's well. The first is to inspect the habitat with a flashlight after it's been in the dark for an hour or so. Immature aquatic insects that have remained hidden from daylight will often be found prowling about in the dark. If a flashlight inspection fails to reveal any activity, carefully move some of the larger rocks or sticks in the habitat; this can be done in daylight or with lights on. If any of your insects remain alive, disturbing their habitat will almost always get them moving. (Caddisflies in their pupal stage of development will, however, be an exception.)

While you shouldn't expect all the insects in your home habitat to hatch, unless something has gone drastically wrong, many will. When you've had an insect emerge and are ready to remove it for examination or preservation, the capture itself can easily be accomplished using the sliding-bottle collecting technique described previously. In some cases, however, you may wish to let a mayfly continue its development until it has completed its dun-to-spinner molt. If so, you may either let the dun remain in the home habitat or transfer it to another cage.

PRESERVING INSECTS

Fly fishermen find many uses for insects they've collected or reared and preserved. Some insects serve as models for pattern designers, fly tiers, or photographers. Others are used by anglers practicing insect identification. All make excellent reference sources.

Two methods are generally used by fly fishermen to preserve insects—dry mounting and preservation in solution. While dry mounting is suitable for preserving insects having solid or hard bodies (for example, crickets or beetles) *all* of the insects that are apt to interest you, especially those with soft bodies, can be preserved in solutions. Because both of these techniques are easy to use, let's briefly discuss each after discussing killing the insects.

Killing Insects

Insects to be preserved must first be killed. For those to be dry mounted, this is best accomplished by gassing. This only requires putting a few drops of ethyl acetate on a piece of absorbent material (but *not* a cotton ball) that's been placed in a small jar. (This should be done several minutes in advance of attempting to gas an insect.)

After the ethyl acetate fumes have accumulated, the insect to be preserved should be released into the jar, and the jar tightly resealed. Gassing will be completed within minutes. Killed insects should be removed from the jar and placed on a dry surface, and the jar lid replaced.

Insects to be preserved in solution may either be killed in the solution or in hot water. Using hot water is best if you intend to examine an insect shortly after it has been killed. If this is the case, and the insect is to be kept as a reference source, it should be preserved in solution immediately after its examination has been completed.

Dry Mounting

This technique involves pinning the body, wings, and legs of an insect to a support base (such as a piece of soft cardboard). Although common sewing pins may be used for this purpose, insect pins, which are longer and thinner, are better. Pins of this type can be purchased from any biological supply house.

Dry-mounted insects are fragile; care must be taken in storing them. Although special glass-covered cases can be purchased for this purpose, a piece of cork sheeting placed inside and attached to the bottom of a shoe box is adequate for temporary storage.

Preservation in Solution

Nothing is easier than preserving insects in solution. All that's needed for temporary preservation is a bottle of rubbing alcohol and some small plastic or glass vials or jars that can be tightly sealed to prevent alcohol leakage and minimize evaporation.

Preserving insects in solution simply involves placing them in the container in which they're to be stored, filling the container with alcohol, and replacing the lid. If the alcohol initially used becomes discolored by insect body fluids, it should be replaced.

When you begin collecting, it's sometimes necessary to store several, perhaps many, insects in a single container. This won't present a major problem *if* you make certain that all the insects in a container were collected at the same time and specific location. If, however, insects captured at different times and locations are mixed in the same container, an almost impossible data recording and analysis problem will be created.

Dry-mounted insects—and the bottles in which those

preserved in solution are contained—should be marked with the date, time, specific location at which the insects being stored were captured, and the collector's name. Those preserved in solution should be inspected periodically to see if additional alcohol is needed to compensate for evaporation.

Preserved insects should, of course, be carefully stored. But this should be done in a manner that makes them easily retrievable for reference purposes.

Before leaving the topic of insect preservation, let me sound another note of caution. Children are usually fascinated by insects. *Store your insect collection, especially insects preserved in solution, out of the reach of children.* You might also wish to consider pasting a *poison* sticker on the outside of the boxes or cartons in which insects are stored. This could save some youngster, and you, a great deal of grief.

4

Data Collection and Recording

Data collection and recording are neither difficult nor time-consuming. But these activities are as important a part of studying angling entomology as any subject we've addressed. Indeed, without a record of the information you've collected, and without documentation describing the results of having tested the angling-related conclusions drawn from your data, it will be impossible for you to apply most of what you've learned from studying this book.

DATA COLLECTION

Because your study of angling entomology is in some respects unique, it's impossible to specify all of the various types of information you'll need to apply your understanding of insect forms and behavior to fly fishing. It is possible, however, to describe most of the data-types you should at least seriously consider collecting and recording.

Time

Noting the month, day, and year when any data are recorded is a requirement. The precision with which "clock time" is recorded, however, depends on the specific type of data being documented. If you simply wish to make some general comments about a particular trip, specifying a range of times such as 9:00 A.M. to 1:00 P.M. will usually suffice. On the other hand, if a particular event is to be noted, such as when a hatch occurred, when a large fish was seen, or insects were collected, then a specific time (like 10:15 A.M.) should be recorded.

Location

Like time, two levels of precision must be considered when specifying location. A general reference must always be provided (such as Big Hunting Creek, Frederick County, Maryland—a stream, county, and state). An exact location, such as the Elbow Pool, must also be identified when insect, pattern, or fishing data are being recorded.

Patterns and Presentations

As we've discussed, patterns may be identified by using specific names (such as a #14 Quill Gordon, dry) or by using physical characteristic descriptions. Whichever approach is selected, make certain the "identifier" will bring to mind the pattern's form (nymph, wet fly, or dry), its size and color, and whether it was tied to float or to sink. Beyond identifying the pattern, note the manner in which

Data Collecting and Recording

a pattern was presented *if* there is something unusual to be remembered. For example, nymph patterns are typically fished below the water's surface. If, however, you had success fishing a nymph that had been dressed to float, that would be an important fact to record.

Insect Forms and Behavior

Like patterns, insects that have been collected or observed may be identified by name, or by their physical characteristics. Notwithstanding the problems that can arise from using informal methods of insect identification, most beginning the study of angling entomology find it easiest to describe insects by noting their hook size, shape, and color. The behavior to be recorded should describe the movements of insects in or on water.

Water Conditions

With the possible exception of information related to unusual conditions, data describing the characteristics of the water at the time you fished or collected insect, pattern, or fishing data (water level, temperature, clarity, flow rate, and the like) are perhaps the most important "conditions" data you can gather. Because water is the medium that links fish and the insects on which they feed, and because they can have such a profound effect on pattern size, color, and presentation decisions, information describing water conditions is especially valuable. Not incidentally, data related to water characteristics provide a better overall measurement of the key conditions that most often affect the success of a trip than will, for example, weather data, since weather is often susceptible to sudden but short-term variations.

Weather Conditions

Though relatively less important than water-conditions data, information indicating air temperature, wind velocity, and direction, and, if available, data describing whether the barometer was steady, rising, or falling are nonetheless valuable. Indeed, it will be weather conditions that most often result in unusual conditions data being recorded.

Unusual Conditions

Data of this type would include notations indicating that at or shortly before the time some pattern, insect, or fishing data were collected, unusual conditions such as heavy rains, sustained high or low air or water temperatures, muddy water from upstream construction, and the like were also noted. Notations like these should warn you that other data collected on the trip where the unusual conditions were found may *not* be typical.

Fishing

Surprisingly, many anglers who record and use data related to their fishing activities often limit the information they record to data describing fish they've *caught*. For data-gathering purposes, this is a mistake. Having data describing when and where fish have been *seen* (caught or not), their species, approximate numbers and sizes is very important. Beyond the fact that such data are useful in trip planning, having them will make you more alert when fishing water in which you know a take is more than just possible.

Special Events

Everything else being equal, the final answer to angling-related questions like, Where should I go fishing? or When would be the best time to fish? may reflect your having documented some special event. By relating "conditions" data—such as time, water conditions, and location—to a special event, like the sighting of a large fish, you may find a direct correlation between the two. And if you can plan a trip where and when those conditions may be recreated, the *event* may also be repeated. Many trophy fish have been caught by fly fishermen who have studied angling entomology and understood this.

References

This is a data-type every fly fisherman studying angling entomology should collect. Don't miss the opportunity to record the names, addresses, and telephone numbers of other fly fishermen from whom you can obtain current information regarding insect activity, water conditions, and the patterns that may be the most effective on water you're planning to fish. If applied, such data will greatly increase the probability of success for any trip.

DATA RECORDING

Fly fishermen make use of a wide variety of forms and formats in recording essential data. Given that there's no rule dictating that one is necessarily better than another, deciding on the forms and formats you'll use is an area where it will pay you to be imaginative. Still, there are some applications-related points you should consider when selecting forms and formats. For example:

- Small log books (with lined sheets) that will fit into a vest or trouser pocket are especially useful in the field.
- While unbound paper data sheets and card files can be used for many purposes at home, they tend to get damaged and lost in the field.
- Maintaining a backup set of data at home eliminates the possibility of losing essential data if the original copy is lost.
- Adopting a format that specifies the data you've decided to collect and establishes the positions on a log or a data sheet where specific types of information are to be inserted will assure that you record essential data each time you collect, and will speed and simplify data analysis. (Two formats, one for a Field Log page and the other for an Insect Data Card are provided. There's nothing special about these formats; they're simply examples of types you can design.)
- Developing different charts that illustrate relationships between various data-types—for example, between emergence times and various mayfly species—will facilitate trip planning and increase the probability of fishing success.

DATA ANALYSIS

It is beyond the scope of this book to address the many techniques that may be used in analyzing data. There is, however, one factor that's so important to remember that I want to emphasize it here. Focus your efforts at data analysis on determining whether the environmental and other conditions existing at, or shortly before, the time some insect, pattern, or fishing data were collected *are substantially the same or significantly different* from those found at the time those data are to be used. The applications value of your data *increases* to the extent such conditions are *similar*. If

DATE: _____ TIME PERIOD: _____ LOCATIONS(s): _____
WATER: Level (High) (Normal) (Low); Clarity (Clear) (Cloudy) (Muddy)
       Flow Rate (Fast) (Typical) (Slow); Temperature _____ (°F)
AIR TEMPERATURE: _____ (°F); BAROMETRIC PRESSURE: (Rising) (Steady) (Falling)
WIND: Direction (N) (S) (E) (W); Speed _____ mph.; Type (Steady) (Gusty)
CLOUD COVER: (Clear) (Overcast) (Rain); HUMIDITY: (High) (Moderate) (Low)
FISHERY:

UNUSUAL CONDITIONS:

SPECIAL EVENTS:

REFERENCES:

Front

The Front and Back of a Field Log Page

Back

PATTERN APPLICATION and INSECT COLLECTION DATA

Name	Form	Size	Color	Site/Time

INSECT DATA CARD #

GENERAL CHARACTERISTICS:

Form:
- o Nymph ( )
- o Larva ( )
- o Pupa ( )
- o Flying ( )

Sex:
- o Male ( )
- o Female ( )
- o Unknown ( )

METHOD OF LOCOMOTION:
_____
_____
_____

Size:
- o Actual _____
- o Hook _____

IDENTIFICATION:

Scientific:
- o Order _____
- o Family _____
- o Genus _____
- o Species _____

Common Pattern Names:
_____
_____
_____
_____

The Front and Back of an Insect Data Card

COLLECTION SITES and TIMES:
_____
_____
_____
_____
_____
_____

HABITAT CHARACTERISTICS:
_____
_____
_____
_____
_____
_____

IDENTIFICATION KEY:
Source: _____
_____
_____

Sequence: _____
_____
_____

PHOTOGRAPHIC RECORDS:
Slide# ( )
Print# ( )
Other: _____
_____
_____
_____

you can remember to apply this concept as you begin using the various types of data you collect, you're going to catch many more, bigger, and smarter fish than you can imagine.

A NEW PERSPECTIVE

Like most anglers who have begun to study angling entomology, you've probably realized that applying a knowledge of insect forms and behavior to pattern selection and presentation decisions will require changing your approach to fly fishing. What you may *not* realize, however, is that developing an appreciation for some of nature's smaller wonders will also *change forever your perception of the world in which you fish*. As Edmunds, Jensen, and Berner so eloquently put it in their book, *Mayflies of North and Central America:*

> Man sees and enjoys nature through his brain more than through his eyes. To walk through a woods or to look into a river without knowing the life that lurks there is comparable to walking through a crowd of strangers. Enjoyment comes with recognition of what we see. One of our friends, a man who had spent many years in an area and knew every road and stream, had not realized that "all those fascinating little bugs" were under the rocks in the stream. His world was much richer after working a week with us in the field.

Having studied this book and the basics of angling entomology, your world is likewise going to be much richer the next time you go fly fishing.

Glossary

The need to recognize and use more precise terminology will quickly become apparent as you continue your study of angling entomology. Anticipating this, some technical terms with which you should begin to become familiar and that relate directly to the text contained in this book are listed in this Glossary. This latter relationship will become evident if you match the numbered symbols with their counterparts in the text.

§1. **Anterior**—At or toward the head or forward part of the body.
  Median—In the middle or along the midline of the body.
  Posterior—At or toward the hind or tail end of the body.
  Dorsal—Top or pertaining to the back or upper side of the body.
  Ventral—Lower, underneath, or pertaining to the underside of the body.

Glossary

§2. Morphology—The study of insect structure.
  Head—The first and most anterior major region of the body.
  Thorax—A major region of the body located between the head and abdomen. (On most insects of fly-fishing importance, one pair of legs will be attached to each of three thoracic segments. Wing pads or wings may also be associated with the thorax.)
  Cephalothorax—The head and thorax considered as a *single* body structure.
  Thoracic—Pertaining to the thorax.
  Prothorax—The first and most anterior thoracic segment.
  Mesothorax—The second (middle) thoracic segment.
  Metathorax—The third and most posterior thoracic segment.
  Abdomen—The third and most posterior major region of the body.
  Abdominal—Pertaining to structures or features of the abdomen.

§3. Simple Eye—An eye with a single facet used to sense light intensity.
  Compound Eye—An eye with multiple facets used to sense movement, color, and the like.
  Ocellus (pl. ocelli)—One or several simple eyes located on the head between the compound eyes of some insects.

§4. Antenna (pl. antennae)—A pair of appendages attached to the head and commonly located between the eyes, usually performing a sensory function.

§5. **Proleg**—A fleshy protuberance projecting from the thorax of some larvae that looks like a leg but lacks the joints of a "true" leg.

§6. **Exoskeleton**—A skeleton or supporting structure on the outside of the body.
Endoskeleton—A skeleton or supporting structure on the inside of the body.

§7. **Metamorphosis**—Changes in a specific insect's form associated with the different developmental stages in that insect's life cycle.
Complete Metamorphosis—A life cycle in which there are four developmental stages (*including a pupal stage* that precedes the adult stage).
Incomplete Metamorphosis—A life cycle in which there are only three developmental stages, i.e., *there is no pupal stage* preceding the adult stage.

§8. **Larva (pl. larvae)**—For insects that undergo complete metamorphosis, the form of an insect in the developmental stage between its egg and pupal stages.
Nymph—For insects that undergo incomplete metamorphosis, the form of an insect in the developmental stage between its egg and semi-adult or adult stages.
Naiad—Gill-breathing, immature aquatic insects.

§9. **Pupa (pl. pupae)**—For insects undergoing complete metamorphosis, the form of an insect in the developmental stage between its larval and adult stages.

Pupation—The process of changing from a larva into a pupa.

§10. **Eclosion**—Hatching from eggs.

§11. **Ecdysis**—Molting.
Exuviae—A cast skin or "shuck."

§12. **Instar**—An insect between successive molts.

§13. **Free Living**—An insect whose immature development does not require it to associate with others of its kin or to maintain a fixed or portable habitat.

§14. **Puparium (pl. puparia)**—A case formed by a larval skin in which a pupal stage of development transpires.
Pharate Adult—A newly formed adult still residing within a pupal skin.

§15. **Emerger**—A nontechnical term describing an immature insect engaged in the process of emergence or "hatching".

§16. **Subimago**—A stage between pupa and adult, e.g., a mayfly dun, which, though capable of flight, is incapable of reproduction.
Imago—The adult or reproductive stage in an insect's life cycle, e.g., a mayfly spinner.

§17. **Oviposit**—To lay or deposit eggs.

§18. **Identification**—The identity of an insect is determined by its structure. To identify an insect precisely requires determining which of its structural features differentiates it, and any insect identical to it, from all other insects. Because insects can be identified with varying degrees of precision, a formal or "scientific" method has been devised which groups insects according to the specific structural features that they have in common. The terms that follow are used in connection with that method.

Kingdom—The highest classification of living things, e.g., the *animal* kingdom.

Phylum—Arthropoda—One of many large groups within the animal kingdom. This group includes crayfish, millipedes, centipedes, spiders, and *insects*.

Class—Insecta—A large group within the Phylum Arthropoda.

Order—A large group within the class Insecta. In this book, four different orders are discussed. They are Plecoptera (stoneflies), Ephmeroptera (mayflies), Trichoptera (caddisflies), and Diptera, an order that includes midges. (Many order names end in "ptera," which in Greek means "wings." In Latin and Greek "di" means "two." The order Diptera therefore includes two-winged flies.)

Family—A large group within an order. For example, within the order Plecoptera (stoneflies) there is a family called Pteronarcidae. (Family names end in "idae.")

Genus—A group within a family. (For example, within the stonefly family Pteronarcidae, there is a Genus called *Pteronarcys*.)

Species—A particular insect within a genus. (For example, within the stonefly genus *Pteronarcys* there is a species called *nobilis*.)

If the insect pictured were to be described using the identification terminology just defined, its description would be

Glossary

Pteronarcys nobilis.

Kingdom = Animal
Phylum = Insecta
Class = Arthopoda
Order = Plecoptera
Family = Pteronarcidae
Genus = *Pteronarcys*
Species = *nobilis*

Since the kingdom, phylum, and class are the same for all insects, references and discussions regarding insect identification focus primarily on order, family, genus, and species.

§19. **Binomial Name**—An insect's scientific name composed of the insect's genus and species. For example, *Pteronarcys nobilis*. (Note that the genus and species names are italicized.)

§20. **Detritus**—Rotted plant or animal matter.

§21. **Detritivor**—An insect that feeds on rotted plant or animal matter.

Predator—An insect that feeds on other insects.

Cannibalistic—An insect that feeds on other insects of the same species.

Bibliography

Of the hundreds of references available to fly fishermen interested in pursuing the study of angling entomology beyond the basics, a few that you may find especially useful are listed in this Bibliography. The references cited are assigned to one of two categories. Those containing information expanding on concepts and procedures like those addressed in this book are categorized as Transitional References. Those concerned principally with the use of insect, pattern, and other data are included in an Applied References category. References identified with an asterisk (★) may be particularly suited to helping you take your next step in studying insects of fly-fishing importance.

TRANSITIONAL REFERENCES

BORGER, GARY A. *Naturals—A Guide to Food Organisms of the Trout.* Harrisburg, PA: Stackpole Books, 1980. (★)

CAUCCI, AL, and NASTASI, BOB. *Hatches.* New York: Comparahatch Inc., 1975. (★)

FLICK, ART. *New Streamside Guide.* New York: Nick Lyons Books, 1969, 1982. (★)

MERRITT, R. W., and CUMMINS, K. W. *An Introduction to the Aquatic Insects of North America.* Dubuque, IA: Kendall/Hunt Publishing Co., 1978.

PETERSON, ALVAH. *Fishing With Natural Insects.* Columbus, OH: The Spahr and Glenn Co., 1956. (★)

RICHARDS, CARL; SWISHER, DOUG; and ARBONA, FRED, JR. *Stoneflies.* New York: Nick Lyons Books, 1980.

SCHWIEBERT, ERNEST. *Nymphs.* New York: Winchester Press, 1973.

SOLOMON, LARRY, and LEISER, ERIC. *The Caddis and the Angler.* Harrisburg, PA: Stackpole Books, 1977.

SWISHER, DOUG, and RICHARDS, CARL. *Selective Trout.* New York: Nick Lyons Books, 1971, 1982.

WHITLOCK, DAVE. *Guide to Aquatic Trout Foods.* New York: Nick Lyons Books, 1982. (★)

APPLIED REFERENCES

ALMY, GERALD. *Tying and Fishing Terrestrials.* Harrisburg, PA: Stackpole Books, 1978. (★)

LAFONTAINE, GARY. *Caddisflies.* New York: Nick Lyons Books, 1981.

KOCH, ED. *Fishing the Midge.* New York: Freshet Press, 1972. (★)

KREH, LEFTY. *Fly Casting With Lefty Kreh.* NJ: Stoeger Publishing Co., 1978. (★)

MARINARO, VINCENT C. *A Modern Dry Fly Code.* New York: Nick Lyons Books, 1950, 1982.

MIGEL, MICHAEL, and WRIGHT, LEONARD M., JR. *The Masters on the Nymph*. New York: Nick Lyons Books, 1979.

OVINGTON, RAY. *How to Take Trout on Wet Flies and Nymphs*. New York: Freshet Press, 1974.

ROSBOROUGH, E. D., "POLLY." (Third Edition) *Tying and Fishing the Fuzzy Nymphs*. Harrisburg, PA: Stackpole Books, 1978.

VENIARD, JOHN, and DOWNS, DONALD. *Fly-Tying Problems and Their Answers*. New York: Crown Publishers, 1972.

WRIGHT, LEONARD M., JR. *Fishing the Dry Fly as a Living Insect*. New York: E. P. Dutton, 1972. (★)

Biological Supply Houses

American Biological Supply Co.
1330 Dillon Heights
Baltimore, MD 21228
(301) 747-1797

Carolina Biological Supply Co.
2700 York Road
Burlington, NC 27215
(919) 584-0381

Bio Quip
Box 61
Santa Monica, CA 90406
(213) 322-6636

Connecticut Valley
Bio. Supply Co.
P.O. Box 326, 82 Valley Road
Southampton, MA 01073
(800) 628-7748

Powell Laboratories
19375 Mcloughlin Blvd.
Gladstone, OR 97027
(503) 656-1641

Ward's Natural Science Establishment, Inc.
5100 West Henrietta Road
P.O. Box 92912   OR
Rochester, NY 14692-9012
(716) 359-2502

11850 East Florence Ave.
Santa Fe Springs, CA
90670-0567
(213) 946-2439

Index

Adult stage, 23, 28, 43
Analyzing data, 80–83
Aquatic insects, 19–40
  behavior of, 38–40
  collecting, 55
  developmental stage of, 23–28
  egg laying behavior of, 33–34
  emergence (hatch) of, 28–33
  habitats of, 19–21
  life cycles of, 21–24
  mating behavior of, 33
  shapes, sizes, and colors of, 36–37
  spinner falls, 34–36

Behavior
  of aquatic insects, 38–40
  data on, 77
  of terrestrial insects, 44–45
Butterfly net, 64

Caddisflies, 23, 25–27, 28, 33, 39
Cages, 65
Case-makers, 27, 28
Collecting insects, 54–66
  butterfly nets for, 64
  in deep or stillwater, 61–62
  equipment for, 59–61
  first steps in, 54–55
  procedures for, 61–66
  in running water, 61
  seines for, 61–63
  site selection for, 55
Colors
  of aquatic insects, 37
  of terrestrial insects, 43–44

Containers for collecting insects, 59, 62–63
Crawling, 38

Data analysis, 80–83
Data collection, 75–79
  fishing data, 78–79
  insect forms and behavior data, 77
  location data, 76
  patterns and presentations, 76–77
  references, 79
  special events, 79
  time data, 76
  unusual conditions, 78
  water conditions, 77–78
  weather conditions, 78
Data recording, 75, 79–80
Dead drift, 38
Developmental stages
  of aquatic insects, 23–28
  of terrestrial insects, 42–43
Dry mounting, 72–73
Duns, 31–32

Egg laying, 33–34
Egg stage, 23, 24, 42
Emergence (hatch) of aquatic insects, 28–33
Ethyl acetate, 72

Fishing data, 78–79
Flight characteristics, 38–39

Habitats
  of aquatic insects, 19–21
  home. See Home habitats
  of terrestrial insects, 19

Index

Home habitats, 66–71
  activating, 69–70
  creating, 66–68
  inspecting, 70–71
  maintaining, 70

Identification of insects, 45–53
  formal method of, 49, 53
  informal methods of, 47–49
  precision in, 46–47
Insects. *See also* Aquatic insects; Terrestrial insects; *and specific topics*
  habitats of, 19–21
  information about, 17–19
  questions to ask to personalize your study of, 15–16
  variability of, 17, 19

Killing insects, 72

Larval stage
  of aquatic insects, 23–27
  of terrestrial insects, 43
Life cycles, 17
  of aquatic insects, 21–24
  of terrestrial insects, 42–43
Location data, 76

Mating, 33
Mayflies, 25, 26, 29–31, 39
Midges, 23, 25–27, 28, 33, 39
Molting, 25–26, 31–32

Nets, butterfly, 64
Nymphal stage
  of aquatic insects, 23–27
  of terrestrial insects, 43

Patterns, data on, 76–77
Presentations, 38
  data on, 76–77
Preserving insects, 71–74
Pupal stage
  of aquatic insects, 23, 28
  of terrestrial insects, 43

Rearing insects, 66–71
  activating a home habitat for, 69–70
  collecting and transporting insects for, 69
  home habitats for, 66–71
  inspecting home habitat and, 70–71
  maintaining a home habitat for, 70
  selecting insects for, 69
Recording, data, 79–80
References data, 79

Seines, 61–63
Shapes
  of aquatic insects, 36–37
  of terrestrial insects, 43–44
Sizes
  of aquatic insects, 36
  of terrestrial insects, 43–44
Sounds, fish's response to, 44–45
Special events data, 79
Species, 17
Spinner fall, 34–36
Spinners, 31–32
Stoneflies, 25, 26, 39
Swimming, 38

Terrestrial insects, 41–45
  availability and accessibility
      of, 41–42
  behavior of, 44–45
  collection of, 55
  life cycles and developmental
      stages of, 42–43
  shapes, sizes, and colors of,
      43–44
Time data, 76
Transporting insects, 69
Tweezers, 62

Unusual conditions data, 78

Water conditions, 77–78
Weather conditions data, 78